THE HUNGRY HEART

THE HUNGRY HEART

Answers
to the
20 Most-Asked
Questions
About Prayer

PIERRE WOLFF

TRIUMPH™ BOOKS
Liguori, Missouri

Published by Triumph™ Books
Liguori, Missouri
An Imprint of Liguori Publications

Library of Congress Cataloging-in-Publication Data

Wolff, Pierre, 1929–
    The hungry heart : answers to the 20 most-asked questions about
prayer / Pierre Wolff.
        p.   cm.
    ISBN: 0-89243-776-6
        1. Prayer—Christianity.   I. Title.
    BV215.W598   1995
    248.3'2–dc20   94-23874
                                                                      CIP

Printed in the United States of America

First Edition

I must dedicate this book
with gratitude
to all people
with whom I shared and lived
its content.
Among them,
first of all,
my wife,
Mary.

Contents

Other Books by Pierre Wolff...

May I Hate God? Paulist Press, 1979. 76 pages.

When we feel any kind of resentment, anger, or hatred, against ourselves, anyone else, or even against God, it is difficult to pray. This is especially true if our religious education was less than ideal. Yet, this book shows that it is possible and healthy to pray even when we are experiencing negative feelings about God. The problem is to know how to pray. *May I Hate God?* suggests a way to use our negative emotions positively in prayer and experience a new closeness with God.

Is God Deaf? Cowley Publications, 1991. 115 pages.

This is a frequent question when we pray! But maybe we are the ones who want to be deaf, or who want God deaf. This book shows that God is always listening to us, and recommends a way of praying that allows us to become aware of what we frequently refuse to hear. It describes the advantages of learning how to be silent and listen to God speaking to us.

Discernment: The Art of Choosing Well. Triumph Books, 1993. 145 pages.

This book applies the method of discernment described in *The Hungry Heart* to specific situations where we have to make decisions. Grounded in Christian spirituality, the method unfolds in a systematic and simple way to guide the reader through the stages of making a choice, whether that choice is by an individual or a group.

God's Passion, Our Passion: The Only Way to Love...Every Day. Triumph Books, 1994. 180 pages.

Moving chronologically through the events of the Passion-Resurrection of Jesus as recorded in Scripture, this book helps us to pray with this portion of the gospels. Praying in this way reveals to us what God as Love is all about, and, therefore, what Love means in every moment of our daily life.

Preface

THE MEDIA usually gives a flurry of attention to religion just before a major holiday. For example, close to Easter Sunday 1994, a famous magazine published an article about prayer. The cover illustration showed a little girl with her hands joined and her eyes turned toward the sky. This illustration suggests some of the classic myths about prayer: that it is an activity for innocent, well-behaved children, chiefly girls; that it is an activity to be performed only at "special" times, when we are collected and serene and can achieve a pious demeanor; and that it is directed to a God who is somewhere "above" us. But if we listen to those who pray frequently, we learn that prayer can be something quite different — and more complex — than these myths imply.

The purpose of this book is not to "correct" the myths symbolized by the magazine cover. Rather, it is to open up to the reader *some practical ways of praying*. So, you will find here, not a treatise about praying, but an explanation of the *means* that help us to pray. Knowledge of these means can lead anyone, no matter how frustrating or empty their previous experience with praying, to a fulfilling, rewarding, and fruitful prayer life.

The idea for this book came from the heartfelt questions of sincere seekers who came to me for spiritual help or attended directed retreats with me. Over the years, certain questions about prayer have been asked so consistently and insistently that I have discerned a pattern from the repetition: It's as if every seeker has the same twenty questions to be resolved before or during the spiritual journey. My responses to these questions, taken as a whole, somehow constitute a theory of prayer.

I am only writing what I have myself received and practiced, and probably in simpler language than you have found in other books and articles. I know that the contents of this book can help people to pray, or to get more out of prayer, because of my own experience and the testimony of others, both laypeople and religious, individuals and groups, whom I have helped. The experts will recognize in these pages what they already know, but this book can nevertheless give them the opportunity to clarify certain configurations of the spiritual journey for themselves.

Each chapter includes a section about prayer with children. I have taught the main ideas and methods of this book to children of all ages for many years. For many children, this teaching has opened up a whole new relationship with God and with the spiritual dimension of life. I have always been surprised by the lack of logic in the way we bring up children. We teach them how to use a fork or a knife, how to tie their shoelaces and comb their hair; but rarely do we teach them systematically *several* methods of prayer, or even a *minimal* means of discernment. We also forget to tell them that activities they enjoy such as drawing, painting, working with clay, etc., can be incorporated into their prayer life and will still be helpful in their spiritual journey when they grow up.

I must emphasize that in this book I am concerned only with the *individual prayer people practice by themselves.* Therefore, I won't talk about the individual's experience during group prayer in a liturgical setting, for instance. Of course, some means of prayer I describe can be used in a group, and indeed my advice on praying with children is primarily intended for groups where adults are helping children to pray.

I am a Christian. So this book will most easily be under-

stood by Christians. However, many of my remarks will be
valid for other believers, and I have seen some of my suggestions work well for Jews (of course, they pray with what
we Christians call the Old Testament). Maybe it is in decoding the messages received through prayer that differences
between diverse traditions appear; still, the greatest mystics
of all religions seem to have had the same experience of God
at the deepest level of their spirituality, and their writings
contain many parallels.

It is important that I leave you with this: Prayer is not ultimately a theory, not even the greatest one. Nobody becomes
a cook merely from reading cookbooks; nobody plays music only by reading a life of Beethoven or an article on the
Rolling Stones. Practice in prayer, as in many things, is the
only way to learn. Therefore, the means presented in the following chapters *must be practiced.* And just as it takes time
for us to master a recipe or a musical instrument, it will
take time for the insights shared here to bear fruit for you.
However, some of my counsel will yield immediate gains —
for instance if you follow my advice about "selecting" and
"staying with it" in Chapter 3, "Why Doesn't Scripture Talk
to Me?" But to reap the full benefit of this book, it will
take weeks or months of practice, and to absorb and put
into your life the whole of what is described in the following pages may even require years. Like a fine wine, the
prayer life becomes richer and mellower with the passage
of time.

The first nine chapters concern some general aids to
prayer and their advantages. Starting with Chapter 10, I
answer some more specific questions to improve each individual's prayer life. But, there again, my purpose is to
reach some concrete suggestions. Also, while writing these
pages, I realized that *all* my books have somehow been about
prayer life.

It is impossible for me to name all the people I would like
to thank for contributing to the knowledge I am sharing here.
And there are people whose names I have never even known

who revealed to me some aspects of prayer life. For example, I am thinking of individuals who impressed me by their bodily posture while we were praying together and others whose writings or songs influenced me. Naturally, I am especially grateful to my own particular teachers of prayer and to all who have shared with me their experiences in prayer. And, of course, I thank Joan.

Chapter 1

Why Would I Pray Formally?

THE ABOVE QUESTION is an important one, despite a modern tendency to prize spontaneity. In *Is God Deaf?* I showed that we are actually praying continually, because some communication always exists between God and us. Some people may maintain that this communication suffices as prayer, making it all the more necessary for me to defend formal prayer.

Praying "formally" means that we set aside a particular moment of our day for entering and keeping ourselves consciously and methodically in God's presence. It implies that we use some specific methods of prayer, like the ones described in Chapter 6, "How Can I Pray? I Don't Know Any Method." And for Christians, prayer is connected with the use of Scripture. So the time and the action of formal prayer are clearly distinguished from all other moments and daily activities. To pray in this way is to enter into a discrete world, even though its ways are very similar to the ways of our ordinary life. Therefore, to pray formally means that we give a specific "form" to our communication with God.

We can say that we have two fundamental ways of praying: one more spontaneous, and the other more elaborate. Some examples of spontaneous prayer might be: I am humming a religious song while driving my car; I let my heart exhale before God what is in me; I am silent in front of a gorgeous landscape or a splendid painting. All of these are valid experiences of prayer. But if I go back later in memory

1

to these moments of spontaneous prayer, I am not likely to find what formal prayer gives me, *information*.

Who Can Tell Me Who I Am?

A primary advantage of praying formally is that this way of praying seeks and yields *information*. Information about what? For instance, I want to know where I am in my relationship with God right now, because I am not sure that I am following God's desire for me. Or, I would like to know God's point of view about a decision I must make. Or, I feel lost and God seems absent to me, and I desire some light. Or, I am impelled to be more faithful to God, but I don't perceive clearly what that means. In sum, I am thirsty for a Promised Land, but I have no idea how to find the right road toward it.

These examples show that we need information: We require something like a map where we can locate our position, our destination, the deviations and the dead ends we have to avoid, the different forks and windings of the road we have to travel. Spontaneous prayer, as good as it might be, will rarely give us such specific indications. If it does, it is going to do so very gradually, more slowly than formal prayer does. Formal prayer systematically gives us information about ourselves, through the methods we use, through the content of our prayers, and through the decoding of our experiences. It also reveals methodically what is leading us, the more or less conscious reasons of our actions and feelings. The more we know ourselves, the more we'll be able to forbid our "underground" or unconscious motivations to lead us. Such knowledge increases our capacity to be really responsible for our actions and increases our freedom. Thus, the value of formal prayer can be summed up in one simple question: Is it not beneficial for us to discover who we are and who our God is, in order to love more, to love better, and to love more freely? For the birthday of people we love, we all ask ourselves, What will they like most? What is the best gift for them, not according to our idea of value, but according to their idea of joy? To answer our question, we both reflect with our mind and ponder with our heart, seeking the gift that will best suit the recipient.

All of this seems to include some selfishness, or at least self-centeredness. It is true that any prayer is always somewhat narcissistic. We have only one personal temple where we can meet God, and it is ourselves. But, if we meet God-Love in our inner sanctuary, we can foresee that the result won't be self-adoration. Of course, the less our prayer is self-centered, the better it is. However, what I said shows that our egotistic tendency here is already a desire to hear what God says through getting information; therefore, it is already an openness to the Other. And this Other always invites us to be open to all others and to act for them. Narcissism is unavoidable, but we can hope that, through formal prayer, it is going to bring forth altruism (We have here a criterion: A prayer life is too narcissistic if it does not open the heart toward others).

The God of Our Childhood

Formal prayer also gives us another benefit, which is that it helps us to know more clearly who "our" God is. Somebody said, "God is an empty notion." Indeed, the meaning of the word *God* depends on what we hear through it. For example, three religions, Judaism, Christianity, and Islam, came from the same roots, but each one emphasizes different features in God. This is true for each one of us. We may all believe in the same God, but as individuals we are more sensitive to or in tune with different specific features of that God. Some of us may ask: "Do we need to know these features?" To ask such a question is to forget that love came to us originally in very specific ways: through the soft hands of our mother, the deep voice of our father, the sense of humor of our oldest sister, or the firmness of our first teacher. These people molded us and also created in us an image of God characterized by security and comfort, humor and a sense of duty, for example. On the other hand, the severity of a mother, the absence of a father, the sarcasm of an older brother, or the contempt of a teacher hurt us and created in us a poor image of God. Our first perception of God is based on the first adults in our life.

Formal prayer allows us to discover more quickly and clearly the childish images we have projected on God. If they were primarily positive, we will be able to cultivate and refine them systematically to our advantage. This will also benefit others, for we will serve them more consciously the way we were served when we were children. For instance, if we understand clearly that our father was gruff but loved us, our own expression of love and our image of God will be gruff as well; but if we stay systematically with the God of Hosea or Isaiah, this will teach us to incorporate tenderness into our love (Hos 11:1–4, 8–9; Isa 49:14–16). If our projections are primarily negative, formal prayer will guide us systematically to purify God's image in us. For example, if the God of our youth looked like a pitiless judge, formal prayer with Scriptures will give us back a God of mercy. Praying in that way, we will be able to answer God's invitations in our life, instead of clouding or distorting them too much with our childhood hurts. I spoke earlier of information: Formal prayer gives us information about our past more methodically than a spontaneous prayer. Therefore, formal prayer gives us more directly the grace to correct, with our new insights, the influences of our past, whether about ourselves or about our God, and to become freer from them.

Finally, formal prayer methodically practiced helps us to discover more easily our intimate Host. Earlier I referred to the use of a map. The methods of prayer and discernment given us by our predecessors, and fruit of their own journey, are like a road map to our inner Holy of Holies. It is up to us to take advantage of such help, and step by step to make our own journey to the core of our own temple, the "temple of the Holy Spirit," as Paul calls it (1 Cor 6:19). Of course,

God's grace can work without all of that. But who would not take a map and learn to read it correctly, in order to go faster by the most accurate way to our Eternal Friend? We are always somehow in exile regarding the One who waits for us in the core of our being. And that is why we might say, thinking of all the help of formal prayer, "I was glad when they said to me, 'Let us go to the house of the LORD!' (Ps 122:1). Who would not listen to God's call to Abraham, literally, "Go for yourself"? (Gen 12:1)

For Our Children

Children are all spontaneity at first, like young animals. But psychologists say that they need some laws in order to structure their psyche and their relationships. This requires a formal education. Everybody learns how to say "please" and "thank you," to eat and drink according to family and social customs and norms. Children find in their families and communities a map for their first steps in life, and therefore also security. Why not give them a similar map for their journey with God? Moreover, children need rites and rituals to establish their sense of security. But they learn essentially by looking at their parents. Thus, if we don't have any personal formal prayer, where are they going to learn theirs?

• A woman I'll call Alice started with me the Spiritual Exercises of Ignatius of Loyola as made in daily life. We reflected about her ability to pray during the weekends, for her two daughters would be at home. She decided to take the risk. She explained to the girls, "When you see that the door of my bedroom is partially closed, it will mean that I am praying to Jesus. Please don't disturb me, except for something very urgent." For a few days, the older, preadolescent daughter passed by and looked quickly at her mother praying, and then she stopped doing it. For several days, the younger one crept into the room. At first, she started by whispering, "Mom, don't worry, I won't disturb you." Then she began to simply enter, and she start playing on the carpet, without speaking, but not without showing curiosity about her mother's activity. One day, she decided not to come anymore. But both daughters knew that Mom had a daily rendezvous with Jesus, exactly as I knew that my mother had one each time she prayed in front of me. And it was not an encounter at Sunday mass in a place and time removed from ordinary life. This encounter took place at home.

I use the above illustration because I believe that praying formally in front of our children is more efficacious than anything we can tell them or teach them about prayer. Our children will believe that it is good to take time for Jesus if they have seen us acting according to our own advice. This being done, it will be our task to find the kind of formal prayer that will fit their age and their sensibility. It goes from reciting a ritual formula with them at bedtime to more elaborate prayers — for instance, the learning of the Lord's Prayer. Chapter 6, "How Can I Pray? I Don't Know Any Method," and Chapter 19, "How Can We Pray, As a Family, As Spouses?," will give us examples of what we can do. As parents and educators, we have a responsibility to give our children a map for their journey toward God, within themselves, in their home. God's home.

Chapter 2

What Is the Use of Praying With Scriptures?

I COULD ANSWER the question with Jesus' words, "Blessed . . . rather are those who hear the word of God and obey it!" (Lk 11:28). But better to give some explanations. Christians cannot ignore Scripture; they are supposed to believe that it is God's Word. So, according to the theory, when we pray with Scripture, we hear God talking to us. However, without dealing with the theological issue of the inspiration of the Scriptures, it is important to explain why and how they can help us in our prayer. I'll give a simple explanation of that.

The Bible contains in its seventy-three books centuries of spiritual experiences in all circumstances of human life. In the Scriptures, we find events concerning family life and also social, economic, and political life. And we see how, through these relationships, the Jews understood the different aspects of their relationship with God. Through time these experiences of faith were shared and discussed, criticized and corrected, analyzed and completed, and transmitted verbally in different communities of believers. Eventually, the whole was written down by many authors. This slow and patient work of generations of believers refined the quality of the texts. Thus, the Bible is an immense encyclopedia of human spiritual experiences, according to many currents of the Jewish-Christian tradition. On a cultural level, it is a priceless treasure for humanity. As Christians, we belong to

this cultural heritage, which originated in some Hebrew no-
madic tribes and was perpetuated for us by the Church. So
it is understandable that we can find ourselves and our own
experiences with God in the Bible.

A Mirror

Scriptures were never written without a reason. They were
written for the instruction of the faithful. For instance, the
gospels were often preached, and later written, to answer the
first Christians' questions. We can imagine a community that
was troubled by persecution and God's apparent silence, and
Matthew saying to them, "Our situation reminds me of that
day when a storm hit us on the lake of Gennesaret. Jesus was
asleep in the boat. Scared to death, we woke him up and . . . "
What followed is in Matthew 8:23–27, and the evangelist
probably invited his listeners to more faith. Or, because many
of the first disciples were Jews, they had to insert Jesus into
their own tradition: So, the explanations for that were all the
Old Testament quotations found in Matthew, for example.
Thus, very often, the Scripture spoken and written was an answer to a particular event experienced by the first hearers or
readers. That text made an explanatory connection between
their situation and the one described by the preacher or the
writer. In fact, all the gospels were (and still are) answering
the questions, "Who was Jesus of Nazareth? Who was, who
is, his God?"

Because of that, when we pray with Scriptures, they reflect for us like a *mirror*. This specific story or person touches
me because, somehow, this relates to what I am experiencing now. It is as if the text I pray with says to me, "You
are Ruth so faithful in her love; you are Martha busy and
jealous of her sister at the feet of Jesus; you are Peter, brag-
ging a lot and falling down later; you are so compassionate
with your mother that you are like the perfume Mary anoints
Jesus with; you are Peter's boat tossed by the waves of your

life, and so on" (Ruth; Lk 10:38–42; Jn 13:36–38; 18:15–18, 25–27; 12:1–11; Mk 6:45–52). Thus, Scripture allows us to identify *where* we are and *who* we are, and therefore *who* our God is right now.

My Brother or My Sister

In fact, the text sends us to one of our brothers or sisters, a person or even an object in the Bible. It might be Isaiah or Jeremiah, Judith or Deborah, Jacob's well or Zacchaeus' tree that has something to teach us. The impact of the text on us tells us that, somehow, we share the experience of the one touching us from centuries ago. But, regarding the story we pray with, we benefit from all the work of refinement accomplished by previous generations of believers. We are introduced into a space always wider than our own experience seems at first sight. If I am denying someone, I am Peter disowning Jesus in the high priests' courtyard; but at the same time, the text puts me under the merciful gaze of our Lord (Lk 22:54–62). Ravished by the transcendence of God, I am like Isaiah, but I am immediately sent to others in order to bear witness as he was (Isa 6:1–9). If I feel like a pile of dry bones, Ezekiel guarantees to me that God wants to revive me (Ezek 37). If I am in a crisis of skepticism, Qohelet welcomes me, but he reminds me also what in life is important (Eccl).

"My" God

So we discover ourselves in praying with Scripture. But at the same time we hear the God we need at the moment we pray. In other words, the Father of Jesus reveals to us the aspect of himself that we have to remember the most right now. I feel abandoned, and God talks to me like a mother through Isaiah (49:14–16). Both of us, God-Joy and I, exult together with the song of Mary (Lk 1:46–55). Repenting, I am coming back to Love, and like a Father who has waited for my return, God rejoices and makes a feast in my heart and in the hearts of those who are welcoming me (Lk 15:11–32). This is supported by the fact that each evangelist and also Saint Paul saw the same Jesus Christ through his own subjective lens (each writer was also influenced by his own community).

But, then, how can we find ourselves among those who might be our brothers or sisters in the Bible? The answer to that question is in Chapter 3, "Why Doesn't Scripture Talk to Me?"

The Better the Knowledge, the Better the Help

Scripture was written centuries ago and in a culture other than ours. So, we won't find all our experiences in the Bible. For example, to my knowledge, only Proverbs 8:30–31 speaks about playfulness. That is not surprising given that our biblical forebears lived in a rural society, where tilling the soil and taking care of domestic animals did not give too much time for leisure. Another example: Laughing is never portrayed positively in the Bible, for it seems connected with irony, mockery, or doubt (isn't it strange that Jesus never laughs in the gospels?). Only one instance of laughter is not criticized in the Bible, Abraham's in Genesis 17:17 (but Sarah's later laughter *is* condemned in Gen 18:12–15) Probably, the Jewish sense of humor was peculiar (it seems that it was rather dry!). Though Balaam and his donkey are undoubtedly amusing (Num 22:22–35), humor is rather subtle elsewhere in the Bible. For instance, the story of the man born blind in John 9 is full of wit, even though the stubborn refusal of Jesus' adversaries will end in a tragedy. Finally, when one of the disciples on the road to Emmaus said to the Risen One, "Are you the only stranger in Jerusalem who does not know the things that have taken place there in these days?" we can picture a smile on Jesus' face! He could have replied, "Oh, I know, firsthand!" (Lk 24:18).

What lesson comes from these remarks? First, the better we know the Scriptures, the more readily we'll find ourselves in them. It is not a question of becoming a scholar but of acquiring a knowledge sufficient to prevent us from distorting the meaning of the texts we use. A better knowledge of the Bible always helps us to find something in the text that is relevant to our life and useful for us. We spend hours studying the time, the milieu, and the style of Shakespeare in order to better understand his tragedies, and of Plato in order to grasp his philosophy. Why should we treat the Bible with less care? People who refuse any serious study of Scripture with the claim that it is God's Word don't see that they have less respect for the Bible than they have for works of literature. In fact, reading the Scriptures always implies some interpretation, and it is best to ground this interpretation on serious study.

For what more directly concerns prayer, I have added at the end of this book an index that was in the first printings of *Is God Deaf?* I have revised it and, I hope, improved it. This index will help us to find ourselves in the Scriptures, especially in the Old Testament.

Years ago, I led a directed retreat with a woman and used the novels of Graham Greene as our text, for Scripture was not working for her at that period in her life. The retreat was fruitful, proving that God can speak through any text. But, with all his talents, Graham Greene could not guarantee to both of us the insights of the Bible, insights accomplished by generations of discerning believers.

For Our Children

Nobody will deny the necessity of introducing our children to Scripture. It is there that they will find Jesus, in whom their parents and educators believe. And we cannot talk about the man of Nazareth without mentioning his roots, the Old Testament. In all of that, children will find the history of God's journey with us, according to the Jewish-Christian tradition. The challenge is to deal with Scripture in a way that is suitable to children.

First, we must remember that *the Scriptures are not a treatise on ethical conduct.* If we forget this point, we make God the Great Moralizer of history, and very often in fact, the Justifier of the norms of our milieu and our time, of our prejudices and preferences. Though I am not certain that this will ever work well with children and teenagers, I *am* certain that it will often backfire. Many people have rejected such a god, while refusing some so-called values recommended by their parents and society. Others have claimed their excesses as right, because they thought that they had the blessing of such a god (for instance, "You shall not kill," in Exodus 20, which meant at the time, "You shall not kill people of your tribe," has justified for some people the killing of "the others").

Scripture is above all the story of the companionship God freely chose to know, and still does with us, through an indestructible covenant. The first and ultimate reality we must help our children to discover in the Bible is that incredible Love who is God, revealed perfectly in Jesus of Nazareth. Therefore, introducing our children to Scriptures must *always* be grounded in this principle, repeated as often as possible: "Let us learn more and more how much God loves us, how much Jesus has loved us." After all, all children like to learn about their past when it proves that they have always been loved, that they will always be loved.

Our task, then, is to make the Scriptures speak to our children today. Here is where we must employ our aptitude to use the mirror I spoke about, our skill to make connections between a biblical story and the child's experience of love now. We'll start by saying, "This story is like us when we forgive our brother or sister," when we comment on a text to young children. Progressively we'll go to "Where do you find something in your life that is similar to this story?" while working with older children.

I still remember what happened during a liturgy for children in a private primary school where I used to help the religion teachers. The text was the parable of the lost sheep in Matthew (Mt 18:12–13), which inspired a child to tell us about his fear while he was lost in a forest and the joy of his parents when they found him. After he shared his experience with the group, it was easy for us to talk about how God is always looking for us with love. The story of Joseph, another day, allowed us to admit jealousy as a human tendency, but also the beauty of forgiveness in God's eyes (Gen 37, 45). And during a Eucharist at home with a group of friends, we were all surprised by Emmanuel, seven years old. He had chosen as a gospel the story of Zacchaeus (Lk 11). At the end of the liturgy, he said to us, "Oh, Jesus went to Zacchaeus' home. But that is exactly like Jesus coming into me at the moment I received Communion."

Chapter 3

Why Doesn't Scripture Talk to Me?

OFTEN THE ANSWER IS, "Scripture does not talk to you because you think that you can pray fruitfully with *any* text. This is not true." Without a method for selecting a suitable reading, finding a text becomes a lottery. The odds of winning are scarce, and that is why, very often, the texts we use are not talking to us.

Christmastime 1963: The liturgies were celebrating joyfully a birth and salvation, inviting Christians to exult. "For unto us a child is born, unto us a son is given," sang the Church. But I could not pray with those texts, for my guts rebelled. The Scriptures quoted by my Church were locked and mute for me. Why? December 26, two friends of mine had lost a daughter, four years old, who had died from a cancerous brain tumor. I had spent the whole night with the family, and early on the morning of the twenty-seventh had helped the mother to put the dead baby in the coffin. For the parents and me, Christmastime was spent talking about the death and concomitant sadness. We were concerned not about the gift of a son but about the loss of a daughter. It was not Christmas for us; rather, it was Good Friday.

We all experience such situations, when the liturgical season does not suit our inner emotions, generated by what is happening in our life. Then we cannot pray with the Church's suggestions, for something refuses them at the deepest level of our being. We can force our minds to find something for us in the liturgical readings — it is always possible — but our heart is somewhere else. The core of ourselves is not where the Church calls us to be. Scriptures do not "talk" to us because they don't really "touch" us in our depths, with an enlivening impact. Following the logic of the last chapter, I assert that *only* the text touching and enlivening us has something to say to us now. Therefore, here are the first two principles of individual personal prayer with Scriptures. They guarantee that we can find a text speaking to us if we do our homework.

Select

Here I am, preparing my prayer time to come (see Chapter 9, "Do I Have to Prepare My Prayer Times?"). I read and reread a few passages of the Bible. But I don't read them with my intellect, to find a message or clarify a historical point, to improve my exegesis or apply the story to my daily life, etc. I read them with my heart. More exactly, I read them *with my guts,* in order to find which one is going to "click," to reach and affect me at the deepest level of myself. I read *several* stories, precisely in order to compare the different impacts of the different texts and see which one is the most powerful for me. And I will pray *only* with the text giving me the strongest feelings deep down within me (i.e., the strongest enlivening feelings. For further explanation, see Chapter 7, "How Can I Decode What Is Going On in My Prayer?"). This text, and this text only, has something to say to me right now, something enlivening. I can and I must forget the other texts, because they have either not too much or nothing at all to offer to me today — for now, they don't touch me. They might have affected me a while ago, they might touch me again someday, but right now they are mute for me. For instance, how could I be in tune with the atmosphere of Holy Saturday, imbued with Love's absence, if the one my heart was yearning for has just said to me, "I love you"?

While selecting, I may find two texts affecting me with almost the same intensity of emotion. I'll take the more powerful one for my prayer time and keep the other for later. Anyway, the chosen text has *already* started to speak, since it has deeply touched me.

What I have described is a usual phenomenon in our lives. A piece of music or a painting, somebody's speech or a movie, a book or a scent, touches us and enlivens us the same way. But this experience depends on the time we give to it. I can already say that 99 percent of the fruitfulness of our prayer with Scripture depends on the accuracy of our selection of a text.

Stay With It

Often we have heard someone say to us, "Please don't interrupt me, let me finish, for you don't know what I am going to say." The principle "Stay with it" is the same invitation in our prayer life. We must stay with the chosen text as long as it is touching us, during the same prayer period but also for the following days. A friend of mine stayed with Abraham's call for a year; another spent three years with Jacob struggling with the Angel (Gen 12; 32). Neither one prayed every day with those stories, but they felt impelled to go back to them once or twice a week to connect the text with their daily life.

This experience is like watching the same movie or reading the same book again and again. During one period of my life, I remained captivated by one specific painting of Matisse and by Sibelius' Second Symphony for quite a while. When we stay with something touching us, we follow the same path, but each time we are on a deeper level, as if we were spiraling down. Each leg of the journey reveals to us something new, as it happens when we see the same opera or read the same novel several times. To pray just once with a text touching us is scratching the surface of what we are called to understand. If we stop midway down, we don't fully harvest what the piece of music or the icon has to say. We must pray till we are sure that we have reached the bottom. Each prayer period is as if we were given one word at a time, and we know the whole sentence when we have received all its words. It is over when the text no longer speaks. What is the signal telling us that our homework is done and that it is time to stop praying with this specific story of Scripture?

One day, I had had my fill of what the movies *High Noon* and *Dead Poets Society* once held for me. All of a sudden, they no longer affected me. We experience the same thing in prayer life. *A text has finished its work when it is no longer or almost no longer touching us.* The clearest signal is when feelings disappear totally: I had always savored some joy with Ruth, and suddenly I just felt *blah* with her story. A less obvious signal is when the feelings are still there, but they are now just "nice." Ultimately uninteresting or insignificant, to the point that we ask ourselves, "So what?" These signals warn us to take another text for our prayer — for instance, the second text we had selected in our list. But it is good at that point to check out the other texts that did not touch us at the moment of our selection, for one of them might work now.

Understanding or Not Understanding

It took a long time before I was fully satisfied by the contemplation of the Russian painter Rublev's icon *The Trinity.* And I never really understood why this painting continued to attract me for years, in spite of all my readings about icons. On the other hand, I *can* explain why to say to God *"Abba"* was powerful and nourishing for me, and how this word was connected with my childhood. Is it always necessary to understand why a text has been good for us? For a century, scientists have been unable to explain perfectly all the benefits of aspirin; fortunately, we have not waited for their explanations before using it. If it becomes clear for us why a text is enlivening us, that's great, because it is useful when we decode God's message to us. If we don't understand everything, it does not matter too much, as long as we let the text feed us. After all, we already know the most important thing: This text gives us life! Many people, with gustative wisdom, enjoy the dish given them and don't ask for the recipe before eating it. Teresa of Avila acknowledged that she enjoyed God's consolations. Let us do the same, chiefly when God does not worry about giving us any explanation. As a matter of fact, psychologists say that we never know at what ultimate depth of our psyche something touches us sometimes, or why it touches us at all. Spiritual authors assert, in religious terms, that only God has access to the core of our being and knows what is accomplished there. So, it is not abnormal if we don't always grasp the reasons for and the meaning of the enlivening impact of Scripture within ourselves.

For Our Children

It is important to help children to become aware of their feelings and verbalize them, and to try to understand the reasons behind their emotions. Thus, children already learn to distance themselves a bit from what affects them, to identify different feelings and to know what to do with them. All of this is an education that is liberating for them. Also, if we share our own emotions with them, children will discover that they are not the only ones to experience certain feelings. We'll assist them in eliminating a guilt complex if the feeling does not seem acceptable, or in alleviating discomfort if the emotion is a surprise because of its newness. And so, here is the way we practiced the content of this chapter in the primary school I mentioned earlier.

1. We prepared the children for the experience of hearing (or reading) the text of Scripture. At least we said, "We are going to hear [read] a story. While we hear [read] it, let us be attentive to what is going to touch us in the depth of ourselves. We might feel joy or sadness, curios-

ity or nothing. It does not matter. After the reading is done, we'll share with each other our impressions." With the youngest children, we merely explained, "We are going to hear a story. Let us listen to it with attention, and see what we are going to like or to dislike in it." Of course, the task is easier when the group consists of children around the same age. But once in a while it is good to have different ages, because "juniors" always look at "seniors," and "seniors" need to see that "juniors" can have the same experiences.

2. Then the text was read. If it was read aloud, the reader used a fairly neutral tone of voice, in order not to influence the children and not to make the Scripture into an operatic aria; this was, for us, an issue of respect for both the children and the Bible. Indeed, the text was a story with some action, and not a discourse of Jesus in John, a chapter of Leviticus or an exegesis of Paul. By the way, the Old Testament is very accessible for children. The choice by Samuel of the "little" David, instead of his big brothers, was especially significant to our children! (1 Sam 16). Of course, we used a translation of the Bible made specifically for children.

3. At the end of the reading, we always allowed for a few seconds of quiet time, saying, "In the silence of our heart, let us remember what part of the story has touched us. In a short while, we'll share about that." Then we started to share our experiences, with no obligation for anyone to do so, with no judgment about what was said (the children were good: They were never angry if one of them stayed silent, nor did they laugh if someone said something considered "funny" by the others). Always some of the adults would share, too, and one day we saw the relief of the children when one of us said, "Honestly, I did not get anything from the story." Sometimes the facilitator would help the children to verbalize their feelings, for instance by suggesting some words to a child who seemed

unable to find the right one. The younger children were asked simply, "In that story, what did you like? What did you dislike?" With the older ones, we went further with three questions: a) Which part of the story touched me the most? b) How did I feel? c) Why was I so touched while hearing [reading] this story? (the rationale of these questions is explained in Chapter 8, "Do I Have to Keep a Journal?")

4. The lesson we extracted from this experience was simply, "See, the words of the gospels [or of the Bible] can touch us." (Further explanation is in Chapter 7, "How Can I Decode What Is Going On in My Prayer?")

Chapter 4

While I Pray, What Do I Do With My Body?

IT IS OUR individual responsibility to educate ourselves (and our children) about managing the body well in prayer. Our churches are rarely the best places for our bodies, for churches don't give us too much freedom when we pray. Of course, in church we pray as members of a social group with standard customs concerning bodily postures. But the pews are set up like ranks of soldiers for an inspection, and we can only sit, stand, or kneel. We don't dance often in most of our churches. On the other hand, the church of the community of Taizé in France invites us to be free with our body: The whole liturgical space is a huge carpet without pews.

The question "What do I do with my body?" often means that our body cramps us. Who has never dreamed about escaping its heaviness? Paul evokes such an experience: "I know a person in Christ who fourteen years ago was caught up to the third heaven — whether in the body or out of the body I do not know; God knows. And I know that such a person — whether in the body or out of the body I do not know; God knows — was caught up into Paradise and heard things that are not to be told, that no mortal is permitted to repeat" (2 Cor 12:2–4). But Paul does not make of his experience a norm, for he mentions it as an exceptional event in his life. So, instead of yearning after such a phenomenon, we must use our body in the best possible way. We cannot

21

escape it, for it is the place of *all* our experiences, even the most spiritual ones. We *are* our body.

We must manage our body with intelligence and care, so that it will faithfully make us present to God. Thinking of the story of Balaam's donkey, I would say that this body that carries us "sees" God with more acumen than our mind (Num 22:22–35). A sort of asceticism, justifiable in cultures other than ours, implies somehow that we despise our body and beat it up as Balaam did his ass. This is unacceptable for Christians: For us, God decided to take on human flesh in Jesus. Paul invites us to treat our body with love, as God's property: "Do you not know that your bodies are members of Christ? ... Or do you not know that your body is a temple of the Holy Spirit within you, which you have from God, and that you are not your own? For you were bought with a price; therefore glorify God in your body" (1 Cor 6:15, 19–20).

Comfortable

Managing our body in prayer requires discernment. The usual piece of advice is similar to the one I explained concerning texts (see Chapter 3, "Why Doesn't Scripture Talk to Me?"). It is simple: *I must find, assume, and maintain the bodily posture that allows me to pray as easily as possible.* And when this posture is no longer helpful, I assume another that facilitates my prayer. Some people would call that complacency. I reply, "Better to be complacent but to hear than to be ascetical and deaf." This is because I still see myself, at eighteen years of age, spoiling two days of my first directed retreat. I had decided to pray on my knees all the time. The retreat master liberated me when he told me what my body had already said, that my physical pain prevented me from hearing God. I also remember a retreatant who knew his most powerful experiences of God while taking baths in a tub. Thus, we must assume and hold the bodily posture that favors consolation, or that helps us the most to endure a time of desolation. And it does not matter which one (For *consolation* and *desolation,* see Chapter 7, "How Can I Decode What Is Going On in My Prayer?").

However, why would God not treat us as we treat our friends? When they are in our home, we say to them, "Make yourselves comfortable." If we are not comfortable in God's presence, what does that mean? Feeling comfortable signifies that we are at ease, in an atmosphere of friendship. That comfort begins with the posture of our body — relaxed but not to the point of slouching.

A Lot of Possibilities

While I was in India, I was captivated by religious dances. Alas, most of the Christian churches in Western countries have lost and not yet been able to reintegrate dance into their liturgies. Fortunately, we have, here or there, some formal attempts to institute liturgical movement and some spontaneous gestures as well. For many Sundays, I had noticed two children in a parish "dancing" during the eucharistic celebrations; both were turning graciously, and one, a "special" child, would also lift up her arms; all of that silently, with the parents' acceptance, but what will these young girls do in a few more years? My body still remembers a mass in a parish in New Orleans where most of the faithful were black people; the entire congregation, including me, swayed together in a kind of restrained dance. One single celebration of a liturgy in black Africa convinces everybody of how much we in the West miss. But, most of us Christians cannot picture ourselves praying through dancing, although dance requires the use of the whole body. However, using our body requires discernment, too.

We must be attentive about what affects our body, and practice what helps us and avoid what disturbs us, while we are praying. Let us forget some retreat houses of old of which the austerity and sometimes the ugliness implied that everybody had already passed through all the mystical "nights" of John of the Cross, and let us adorn the *space* where we pray. We do that for the place where we meet our friends, for love is fed by this kind of attention: flowers, music, and the perfume of potpourri in the living room; soft light or lit candles, tablecloth and embroidered napkins in the dining room; appetizing smell coming from the kitchen where lovingly concocted dishes wait for us. All this luxury allows the encounter to assume all its dimensions. Can we do the same with and for God?

CARE FOR OUR EYES

In Chapter 6, "How Can I Pray? I Don't Know Any Method," I speak of objects we can contemplate. Pictures, paintings, statues, icons, bouquets, and such make our prayer easy. A room with pleasant and calming colors, a window with a view on a splendid landscape, do the same. We can also play with light and darkness according to our own sensitivity and what we are praying about. A lit candle can change many things; nighttime or dawn can be a grace. Each one of us has to discern what is the most suitable for himself or herself, what helps without creating too many distractions.

CARE FOR OUR EARS

Music or songs might inspire. They can even be directly what we pray with or about. They can make the beginning of our prayer period easier, or wrap up at the end the time we have spent with God. But let us remember that silence usually becomes the best companion in this kind of encounter, exactly as it is often the most delightful enjoyment with a friend.

CARE FOR OUR NOSE

Incense has been burned in the celebrations of many religions for many centuries. For me, the association between prayer and scent was made at home: My mother liked to pray in front of us with the smoke and the smell of incense. I won't list here the meanings given to such a practice, for I just want to emphasize what is connected with our sense of smell in prayer. The atmosphere of a room is changed by the scent of a bouquet. So can our prayer be. Mary anointed Jesus, and "the house was filled with the fragrance of the perfume" (Jn 12:3).

CARE FOR OUR SENSE OF TOUCH

Our whole body has the sense of touch. A room covered by a carpet calls our body to sit, to lie down on the belly or the back, to take Yoga postures, to be on our knees, etc. The list of possible bodily positions, and their significance, is endless. Praying barefoot suggests humility or poverty, for instance, whether we stand or walk gently or dance. And, of course, we can use our hands, and hold a crucifix, or a statuette of Jesus' mother (as does one of our little neighbors, eight years old, when she comes to our place. I just told her what I had written about that, and she admitted that "somehow, it is like a prayer."). After all, it is with our hands that we hold or caress, and that blind people discover our face.

CARE FOR OUR MOUTH

In some traditions, prayer includes the use of hallucino-genic herbs (do we have this behind the prophets' frenzy in 1 Samuel 10?). The mouth, as the organ of eating and taste, is often mentioned in the Old Testament (what would life be like without the sense of taste?). It was a part of prayer when the victim of a sacrifice was eaten (Lev 3). For many Christians, the eucharistic meal reaches its highest point when they receive the Bread-Body and the Wine-Blood of Christ. But I think of the mouth especially as the organ of speech. To pray aloud is sometimes powerful, for *we hear ourselves talking* to God. Singing, humming, repeating a mantra made with our own words or words from Scripture, and saying the rosary are a few examples of using our mouth in a personal way; in fact it is an individual application of what has characterized monastic prayer in many religions.

Such use of our five senses goes further than keeping our body materially busy. A long Christian tradition has always taken them seriously, according to the logic of the Incarnation seen in many texts of the gospels, and for instance, in John's epistle, "what was from the beginning, what we have heard, what we have seen with our eyes, what we have looked at and touched with our hands, concerning the word of life" (1 Jn 1:1–3). And this tradition speaks about five "spiritual" senses, rooted in our five bodily senses, and asserts that they allow us to experience the Risen Christ within ourselves — "in our soul," some people would say. Through a very intimate experience of faith, he becomes Light, Word, Perfume, Touch, Bread and Wine. Another dimension of our life as human beings is *time*. I speak about it in Chapter 5, "How Long Must I Pray?"

Distortions

Our attempts to use our body in prayer are not always successful. First, because we often don't know or are too lazy to find out what is really helpful for us. Second, any use of our body can distract us from the first goal of prayer: to get in touch with God. I won't say that enjoying a melody or a lovely scent, taking the lotus posture or holding a crucifix, singing or contemplating an icon, are not prayer in themselves. They might be, chiefly if they take place in the time consciously devoted to prayer. But our attention might be so much focused on the means itself that God is forgotten (this might even be a sign that we don't really want to hear God). Finally, some bodily experiences can be so powerful that they become a problem, at least for people belonging to the Jewish-Christian religious culture. Eating hallucinogenic herbs, using techniques that provoke trances or even ecstasy, create for me questions like, "What exactly are we looking for through that? How much are we still ourselves? And, therefore, who is the God implied in these practices?"

I am not a whirling dervish, and so I cannot say anything about such experiences of spinning on oneself. But I am a bit skeptical about some kinds of bodily excitements described by persons with whom I share a culture.

Somebody We Don't Know
or Somebody We Have Forgotten

Nobody can tell us what body positions are appropriate for us — only our body can tell us that. And our body is right when it tells us which specific posture we have to take. It wants to talk about some deep things. This is why I say to people I help spiritually, "While you are praying, follow and trust your body." When we give our body the freedom this chapter recommends, we make some discoveries concerning ourselves.

First we get in touch with someone we don't know very well, even though it is ourself. One example will explain what I mean. I have known some persons, including myself, who had the possibility of making a retreat by themselves, alone in a place loaned to them by some friends. They had decided to follow their body, not only for postures in prayer but also for the schedule of the day. Quickly, the length and the number of prayer periods changed, the day started and finished earlier or later, fewer meals were necessary, everything slowed down, etc. They experienced what some people knew through scientific experiments of speleology, when they volunteered to spend months underground. The discovery is that our body has *its own pace*, which deserves some consideration because it is rarely respected by us in our daily life, often to our detriment. So, with its freedom, our body reveals someone we ignore too much. Also, our body can reveal someone we have forgotten.

When our body feels free, it often speaks about things that have been carved in it for a long time, since our childhood. For instance, our body remembers aloud the wounds or the gratifications we have no longer been conscious of. Already, a restless body says a lot about our inner irritation or impatience. In prayer, our body can express more freely the pains or the fears, the ruses or escapes, the caresses or tendernesses, experienced in the past by the child who is still within us. So, when we follow with trust the inspiration of our body, whatever desires to emerge can do so, and at the same time, what God desires to say about it can emerge as well. And this will work even better if the text we pray with has been selected correctly. A retreatant told me that, from prayer period to prayer period, his body was opening itself more and more: fetal posture first, then lying on the back, then wide-open arms and hands; and, simultaneously, the man opened himself more and more to what God was saying through the selected text. Another told me, "As soon as I prostrate myself, I am seized by awe and adoration."

I can now talk about praying *naked*. Some people in retreat with me told me that they had done that. I noticed, when they explained their experience, that the desire to pray that way must come from our gut, and not from our mind. The body wants to express *symbolically* things like, "Lord, here I am, before You, naked, just as I am, or, accepting my manhood or womanhood, or in all my poverty and vulnerability, or not trying to hide myself from You, etc." This way of praying never created problems (as long as privacy was protected by a closed door!). On the other hand, the experience of people who had decided with their mind to pray naked was different. They realized quickly that they were merely indulging their own sensuality.

For Our Children

Our children must know that they can pray through dance; at least by themselves if there is no opportunity to do so in our churches. But in any case let us teach them the management of their bodies, with the same principles as those above but adjusted to their age. We must emphasize that

God has no preference for any specific posture, including the standard ones that make children restless in prayer. Soon enough, they'll know the customs of their religious culture about bodily postures. But it would be sad to make them believe that social norms about the body in prayer define intimacy with God. Sorrow for our sins can hit us while we are sitting down, and is not necessarily linked to kneeling. A great spiritual joy may not be best expressed by lifting up our arms, and may even make us prostrate. In the primary school, we always celebrated on the floor, and around a low table for the eucharistic liturgy. The atmosphere, the behavior of grown-up people present, invited all of us not to slouch on the carpet. We always reminded everybody that it was polite not to disturb our neighbor by being unquiet with our body (we gave the example of being annoyed by somebody beside us in a movie theater). I have never seen one child behaving in a way unbearable for others.

In the school, we found many means to keep the children's eyes, ears, noses, sense of touch, and mouths captivated. We often worked for the joy of almost all our senses, but sometimes we focused on only one: for instance, to have the children look attentively at one painting, to listen carefully to the words of a song, etc. The possibilities depend on the creativity of the helpers and sometimes of the children themselves. It is important to tell them that they can do the same when they pray, alone with God (by the way, I talk with adults only about praying naked, for the topic would make many teenagers feel ill at ease, while younger children would think that it can be done anywhere). And we never forgot to remind children that it was better never to do some things when they were alone: the best examples being to light a candle and to burn incense!

When children play a story of the gospels, they enter with their whole body into the text. To make the Stations of the Cross is easy. Seeing children pray like this shows that it is not our intellect that puts us in touch with God, for they are before us *all* eyes, *all* ears, etc. And something happens within them, some experience of God. Joan, eight years old, curls herself around her knees silently for a long while after receiving the Body of Jesus; after the service, I said to her, "I saw you. I was impressed by your posture. I suspect that something happened to you." "Oh, yes," she replied. Later, her mother said to me, "Did you see my daughter? I am sure she experienced something." "Only God can say," Paul would say (2 Cor 12:2–4).

Finally, without making a big deal about it, distractions are an issue with children. We must simply center the prayer on the main theme, again and again. For older children and teenagers, it would be good to talk about that with them (see Chapter 13, "What Can I Do When I Am Distracted in Prayer?").

Chapter 5

How Long Must I Pray?

A S HUMAN BEINGS, we live in time, and so we must take time into consideration in our prayer life. Things have a beginning, a middle, and an end, and they endure. Any creation occurs only after some preparation, let us say a pregnancy, from a flower to a piece of fruit, from an egg to a baby. We have to know if we can make it, and how long we can accept to be pregnant to get a beautiful baby at the time of delivery. We need and take time to enjoy our friends' presence, as often and as long as necessary for our friendship. We select the best moments of the week and the day, in order to make the encounter enlivening. If someone is tired, we shorten the visit. We are sorry if we have not seen each other for weeks (if not, what is the meaning of the so-called friendship?). We forget to apply these ordinary experiences to our prayer life. So, let us wisely, lovingly, and freely take time with and for God. Here again, discernment is necessary, for we have to find what fits us individually.

The Right Time

The question "How long must I pray?" is wrong. The right one is, "How long *can* I pray?" If we are not trained, praying too long will just make us tired and become burdensome. Being with God won't be pleasurable. However, there's a saying that goes, "Time needs time." If we don't give ourselves the right length of time, nothing really deep will happen. Ex-

31

cept when we are in a hurry, we don't like to meet a friend for
five minutes only! The maximum time to spend with God, according to the best spiritual authors, is around one full hour.
To pray thirty minutes already allows us to make discoveries,
chiefly if the preparation and the selection have been serious
(See Chapters 3 and 9, "Do I Have to Prepare My Prayer?"
and "Why Doesn't Scripture Talk to Me?"). This is to take
the time. Indeed, this might still be too long for beginners.
So they will start to pray for five minutes, then for ten, and
progressively reach thirty minutes. This is to take *our* time.

The picture above is also influenced by our answer to the
question "When is the right time for me?" Some people are
early birds, easily up and immediately alive. Others are sleepy
till midmorning. We guess for which ones it would be better
to pray at the beginning of the day. Some others function very
well late in the day; it is probably at that time that prayer
would be more fruitful. Usually, we feel heavy after meals,
and not in a great shape when we are tired: We may avoid
these moments. If we take the best time of the day for us, we
can expect an easy and lasting prayer. We have also to take
into account the daily schedule of our other activities, for we
are not monks whose life is all structured around prayer (see
Chapter 14, "How Can I Pray When I Am Too Busy?").

It is good to have a prayer period the beginning and the
end of which are *clear-cut*. Spiritual authors recommend we
start by "putting ourselves in the presence of God" and finish
by saying a formal prayer like the Our Father. It is true that
we cannot start praying without reminding ourselves Who
we are going to deal with, without awakening our faith. It is
healthy to know how to say clearly "Hello" and also "Good-
bye." This eliminates questions that some people would ask
themselves if they are threatened by scrupulosity and a guilt
complex. To fulfil, even materially, only the contract we've
made with God is already something very positive. After
all, even though it might not have been perfect, we came,
we were there, we stayed till the last minute. And it will
be difficult for lax people to excuse themselves if they have

not respected the contract. The fox imagined by Antoine de Saint-Exupéry said to the Little Prince, "But if you come at just any time, I shall never know at what hour my heart is to be ready to greet you.... One must observe the proper rites," and then he explains this last word: "They are what makes one day different from other days, one hour from other hours."* No question, God's heart is always ready, but a minimum of rite helps ours, and makes one hour different from other hours.

Full of Greed or Without Generosity

Concerning time in prayer life, we have a simple and wise piece of advice. It has no meaning when we are grasped by God through a powerful consolation, because we are no longer aware of time. One hour passes like three minutes. If it happens to us, let us just enjoy God's grace with gratitude. But usually we are conscious of time, and we should keep in mind this: *If praying is delightful, it is better not to stay longer than the decided time; if it is a little hard, it is better not to shorten the decided time, but even, on the contrary, to stay one or two more minutes in prayer.*

The first statement concerns the famous "spiritual greed." When we are consoled in prayer, we like it. The temptation is then to stay longer to relish the treat given us. God is not offended, but it means that we have gone surreptitiously from our interest in the Giver to our greed for the gifts. What a love! We become like a child so fascinated by an ice-cream cone that he forgets everything around himself, and first of all his benefactor. When we stop our prayer at the moment we originally decided on, we are in effect saying to God, "Of course I like your gifts, but I came for You and not for them. I want to prove this to You and to myself; so I stop praying, even though it is delicious." When we eat too much of a

---

*The Little Prince (New York: Harcourt, Brace and World, 1943), 67–68.

good dish, we risk feeling our stomach swell like a balloon; when we become spiritually greedy, it is our head that may swell! This explains why spiritual authors recommend that we stay humble when we get consolation. Also, we risk producing exhaustion, being trapped by childish self-adoration, or becoming addicted to prayer as to a drug. I have myself met some people who behaved like prayer addicts.

The second statement sounds like the motto of masochism or machismo: "It is painful. Great, let me enjoy it longer, you'll see how strong I am!" Because we are invited to stay for only one or two more minutes, we don't give room to any morbid tendency or to macho pride. When I said, "One or two minutes," I repeated exactly what was said to me by excellent spiritual masters. But, outside of fighting masochism or machismo, what is the value of the advice? Psychologists who know Freud's Principle of Reality ("Life does not always satisfy our needs") would find this counsel very wise. One or two minutes of extra prayer time is too brief a period to indulge the masochist or macho man in us, but it is long enough to train us to endure frustration. We'll learn how to face, how to manage, and how to pass through dissatisfaction in prayer; and, slowly, this capacity will impregnate all other fields of our life. But eventually we can look at the advice on another level and say, "Who would not like to give one or two more minutes to a friend? What love would refuse one or two more minutes to God?" And it also reminds us of Jacob saying to the Angel, "I will not let you go, unless you bless me," or, "Give, and it will be given to you. A good measure, pressed down" (Gen 32:26; Lk 6:38).

Consistency

There is another question concerning time in prayer: "Must I pray every day?" If we look at monks, who are the specialists of prayer life in any religion, we answer, "Of course, yes." If we can do so, so much the better, for we know people well only if we are with them frequently, and this is true of our relationship with God, too. Also, if a love expresses itself once a week only, we might have some questions about it. I know laypersons who, as busy as they are, pray for one hour a day; so it is not impossible. Some people would say that it is just a question of self-discipline. I cannot associate the word *discipline* with Jesus' God, for it reminds me of the first words of the Code of the French Army: "Discipline being the main strength of army...." I won't deny the value of effort in life, but I prefer to say that praying daily is a matter of being organized for the sake of love. For it is a well-known fact that when we fall in love with someone, we always find time for the beloved, and we are able to organize our schedule accordingly. And the more we spend time with the beloved, the more consistently we want to do so.

This consistency is absolutely necessary if we want to discover clearly what God says to us. Once in a while, a very strong spiritual experience reveals God's message for us in the twinkling of an eye, but this is not at all the usual way. God respects time, which is part of creation, and speaks through it. Let me use a comparison: The fruit of each prayer period is like one single word of a phrase we don't know yet; time and the addition of many prayer periods, and thus of many words, will give us the whole sentence God wants to say. Then we can understand God's message. This is treated in Chapter 7, "How Can I Decode What Is Going On in My Prayer?"

For Our Children

What I said can be applied to teenagers. For younger children, we must distinguish whether they are by themselves or in a group.

A child is able to spend a long moment alone while humming a religious refrain, contemplating a picture about the gospel, remaining silent in a chapel he/she likes, etc. Children really appreciate when we say, "Take the time you want,"

for this respects their freedom. So, when children are in the
mood to pray alone, let us leave them free. They will stop
when things no longer inspire them. Let us foster such a
habit by leaving our children alone, for instance, in a chapel
where they feel secure and quiet, when they are worshiping
after receiving the Body of Christ, when they admire a religious picture they like, when they are in bed, after we have
suggested to them to pray before sleeping. When my little
neighbor takes the statuette of Jesus' mother in her hands,
I always leave her alone in our rocking chair. The oratory
of the primary school was perfect for the children's special
moments of grace. Those moments are the child's and God's
mystery; but they depend on our help (and our example).

In a group, the question of timing is connected with three
things.

1. The physical and emotional condition of the children (too
   excited or too tired, a too heterogeneous group, a place
   not made for children, etc.).

2. The quality of the time spent in prayer. This requires
   adults who know how to captivate and keep alive children's attention (I remember storytellers to whom children listened with their mouths agape for longer than
   thirty minutes!).

3. The ways we allow them to be a part of the service. When
   these conditions are realized, we must simply keep the
   prayer centered on the same theme, repeated creatively
   during the whole celebration.

If not, better to be short, and sometimes very short. Indeed, I remember making the Stations of the Cross with a
group of children. After an hour and a half, they wanted
more! Of course, it was their first time, and we sang, read,
walked, interceded, etc. It was a "passionate" trip through
the Via Dolorosa. But also, I still see twenty kids rushing into
a church, kneeling around the altar, saying together aloud a
short prayer suggested by the woman who was with them.

Then, she said, "If some of you want to stay longer, it's okay. Take your time. You'll join the group outside in the backyard." Most of them fled like a flock of sparrows. Three or four stayed, silently, for a few more minutes, then left. I was moved, for who knows? But who would not help little children?

Eventually, if we intelligently raise our children to pray, so that prayer is not a burden to add to their homework, it will be easy to invite them to pray regularly. If praying with the family, or in a group, has been interesting, our children will more readily desire to pray by themselves. A discreet reminder to pray from us is not out of order. But, ultimately, this has to be their free choice, and we cannot force it. The issue here is their relationship with God, which will not brook tactless interference. We can try to encourage our children to sate their hunger for the intimacy of the One who did *not* say, "Force the children to come to me," but "Let the little children come to me; do not stop them" (Mk 10:14).

Chapter 6

How Can I Pray?
I Don't Know Any Method

——— ◆ ———

P
RAYER LIFE is often difficult because we know only one
or two methods of praying. But if we cannot do everything with only one tool, we can also be encumbered
if we have too many tools! So it is helpful to have learned
and practiced a few methods and found which ones fit us the
best. Three fundamental ways of praying summarize the diverse methods. They are: to pray with a *notion,* or a *picture,*
or a *melody.*

Praying with a Notion

The word *notion* emphasizes that this method primarily uses
our *intellect.* Strictly speaking, it is often called *meditation*
by specialists.

The Work of the Intellect

We have selected a text that touches us, and now it is time to
pray. Starting our prayer period, we slowly read and reread
the text. Then we reflect about its content, through four
questions, more or less like these:

1. What kind of God is described in the text? For instance,
   which adjectives would I use to name the being of this

God? A tough and angry God? A compassionate and merciful God? A hidden and humble God? And so forth.

2. What kind of human being(s) do I see in the text? I can still try to find the right adjectives: arrogant, defiant people? Poor, sad persons? And so forth.

3. What kind of interaction is taking place between the action of that God and the action of the human being(s)? A relationship similar to contrition-pardon, or plea for a miracle and thanksgiving, or mutual love, or sin and punishment, or distress and comfort, etc.?

4. What kind of similarities can I find between my discoveries through the text and my daily life? For example: Jonah is sent east by God, and he goes west (I am escaping a situation begging for my presence and my witness); Balaam beats up his donkey that sees the Angel of God (I am spending my time damaging my body, though it is giving me many warnings, telling me to stop). (Jon 1:1–3; Num 22:22–30).

We can also do an equivalent of that with a prayer of the Church we know by heart, like the Lord's Prayer. We take each word or phrase, we reflect on it for a short while, just in order to obtain insights, and we go to the following one. And, if one word or one phrase grasps us, we can stay with it as long as it is fruitful. We may also use our intellect to pray with our sins or the news of our life, in a sort of examination, but this is treated in chapters 10 and 11, "Can I Pray With the News?" and "Must I Pray About My Sins?"

We must notice that a *previous* study of the text of Scripture will make it more nourishing and fruitful and will remove some questions that could block the prayer (historical, geographical, cultural, information that might illuminate the text). I said "previous" because praying has nothing to do with studying the Bible (see Chapter 9, "Do I Have to Prepare My Prayer Times?").

The Colloquy

Studying the text could make us miss the desired goal, which
is the colloquy. All spiritual authors say that the intellect op-
erates only in order to prepare the next step, usually called
colloquy. This is the moment when our heart, pushed by the
discoveries of the intellect, feels impelled to talk to God and
express what now dwells within ourselves: feelings, desires,
petitions, intercessions, and so forth. The goal of the intellectual work is to lead us to the colloquy. So, as soon as our
heart speaks, we stop reflecting. It is only when the heart has
nothing more to say that we come back to the work of our
intellect in order to go further in our reflection, in the text,
till another colloquy comes. The colloquy being the goal of
prayer, it is okay if it takes over the whole prayer period. We
don't have to be disturbed to see our intellect doing nothing,
for as a matter of fact it has achieved, and very well, what it
was intended to accomplish.

This method can be practiced with any text, for our intellect always finds something anywhere, and very easily if the
selection and the preparation have been done seriously.

For Our Children

The above method can be used, as described, for older children. With younger children, it is be better to discuss the
questions with them. It is easy to say, "How does Jesus act
in this story?" "What is this man or woman doing, or what
have they done?" "What happened in this story, if you compare the beginning to the end?" "Does all of that remind you
of some things in your own life?" If we pray with a prayer
of the Church, the question can be, "Father, give us our daily
bread, what does that mean for you?"

For the youngest children, it will be enough to tell them
the story and to extract from it what concerns our life, but
chiefly Jesus' and God's love for us. Thus, the task is to help
children reflect on God's behavior in the face of our actions,

through Jesus, if he is in the text. The colloquy can be left to the children's initiative or expressed aloud for and by the group. Even with young children, I have always given them a few seconds of silence, after saying, "Now, say to Jesus what you want, maybe because of the story, silently in your heart for a few seconds." I believe that they have their own word for God, and that God enjoys it like a treat.

Praying With a Picture

The word *picture* means that this time we pray with the help of our *imagination* (our capacity to make mental images). This method is sometimes named (*evangelical*) *contemplation*. It happens in this way.

1. We start by reading and rereading the text we have selected because it was touching us. But we don't read it with our intellect, in order to find a message, to understand God's motivations, to apply the verses to our daily life, etc. We read the text exactly as we would read any kind of story we would narrate later to some children. We just try to put into our memory the story of the text, with its details (often, this kind of reading reveals to us things we had forgotten or never noticed, for example, in John 19:20–29, Thomas wants to touch Christ's wounds but does not do it when Jesus is in front of him).

2. When the story is sufficiently engrained in our memory, we visualize with our imagination the action, as if we were present there at that moment. And, still with our imagination, we put ourselves into the story. This can take two different forms.

3. We can become *a spectator or an actor.*

As a spectator, we are really present to what is going on, seeing and hearing it, and so forth. But nobody is noticing us, because we are like one anonymous person there. If our selection was well made, becoming a spectator is easy, and we can even try consciously to be so.

To become an actor is quite different. Here, I want to emend and complete what I wrote on too briefly in my book *Is God Deaf?* Usually, to become an actor means that, without warning, we *are* all of a sudden one of the characters of the action, person or thing. I am the prodigal father of Luke 15 welcoming the repentant son back home, I am Jesus curing a mute man in Matthew 9, I am one of the persons bringing down Jesus' body from the cross in John 19. Or I am the empty bucket of the Samaritan woman in John 4, the perfume poured out by Mary in Bethany in John 12, or the almsbox called "the treasury" of Luke 21 where the widow puts her two little coins. The meaning of what is happening to us is clear enough, it is an *identification.* The text works here like a *mirror* (see Chapter 2, "What Is the Use of Praying With Scriptures?"). It says to us, *"Right now, you are this one."* Because at this specific moment of our life we open our arms and our heart to somebody coming back to us, we are helping another person to express things hidden for a long time, we are taking care of a brother or sister badly wounded by some event. Or, the text reveals to us that we accept a lifestyle that keeps us empty, that we dispense lavishly our compassion for someone in need, that we are a treasure in God's eyes although we have not too much to offer.

To become an actor cannot be provoked by will, even goodwill! Some retreat masters sometimes say, "Put your feet in the Father's, in Peter's, in Mary's shoes." This does not work, and the risk is to pretend, because we never know exactly who we are right now in God's perspective. Only God knows it and can reveal it through the symbols used by the Bible.

We must not be surprised if sometimes this contemplation-mirror sends us back to events of our childhood. When this occurs, the biblical story can even disappear from our experience, and we can just go back into what emerges within us from our past (in terms of feelings at least, for we have to be careful not to take as historical what can come back to the conscious level of our mind). That means that, in the current situation, it is the child within us who is reacting. The best is to let the contemplation work (we'll have to interpret the message later. See Chapter 7, "How Can I Decode What Is Going On in My Prayer?"). Also, it is important to remember that each one of us has a peculiar kind of imagery. For some people I have helped, the images were rather musical or pictorial, for others visual. And, when the one we get is fading away, we go back to the text and start the same process again. It is not necessary here to mention the colloquy, for it comes out spontaneously during the story, if it has to. This method works with both the Old and New Testament, as long as the selected text includes some action. Finally, the connection with Scriptures saves us from dealing with symbols void of a clear reference to God or Jesus, and helps us when we decode the spiritual message connected with this past or present perceived in the mirror of God's own Word.

A very systematic way of contemplation exists, and it goes further. It is usually described as *the application of the five senses of the imagination.* It means that we try methodically and successively to see, hear, smell, taste, and touch what is in the scene. This works well for some people, and indeed it involves the whole being in prayer. Contemplating can take many forms, like making the Stations of the Cross, saying the rosary while contemplating evangelical scenes, etc. Contemplation belongs to an old tradition, for our ancestors, who made the stained-glass windows, the frescoes, and the statues of the cathedrals of the Middle Ages, wanted, in part, to facilitate the contemplation of the faithful, chiefly those who could not read.

For Our Children

Contemplation is a wonderful form of prayer for children, whose imagination is always ready to function! We have only to teach them that they can use it to be with Jesus. For teen-agers, the method can be taught as it was described above. For the youngest children, contemplation will be any prayer using images. I have already mentioned a way of the cross made with a group of children. It worked very well because we had to look at images, to discover their structure through some brief explanations, to walk between two stations, to sing, to intercede, etc. It was a way of applying our senses. To pray in front of the Nativity scene with the Infant, Mary, and Joseph is a piece of cake. To visit a church and contemplate the stained-glass windows easily becomes a prayer.

The only caution is not to overstimulate the children with too many things and too many details. For instance, they should play with pictures that are not too complicated or sing very few songs or repeat the same refrain, in order to center the prayer unceasingly on one theme only. Moreover, this lets them know that grown-up people *also* pray like this. So, when they grow up, they may still use the same method and not think that to pray with the imagination is just "kid stuff." They will also keep forever a certain respect for their imagination, when it is well governed. After all, artists are the proof that imagination has value.

Praying with a Melody

The word *melody* signifies that this way of praying plays with *repetition* and *rhythm;* it employs a mantra, like a melody. This method exists in many religions. I saw it practiced spontaneously by a child with Down's syndrome. Before his parents, who were moved and full of awe, he used to say again and again, for weeks, the same prayer before falling asleep: "God is great, God is great." We never knew what he meant. God certainly did.

The method works like this: We take the text we have se-lected and reread it with attention in order to select in it the one phrase touching us the most. And we repeat this phrase endlessly. We don't try to understand or to analyze anything, or to contemplate anything that could be suggested by the sentence. We repeat the sentence. This method became famous as the "Jesus prayer" when it was reinvented by some Russian starets in the nineteenth century. But they used only the words of Bar Timaeus, "Jesus, Son of David, have mercy on me!" (Mk 10:47). *The Way of a Pilgrim,* of which the writer is unknown, describes it beautifully. I suggest repeating the phrase that touches us today, and not only the one of Bar Timaeus. Following the logic of what I mentioned about applying the five senses, this method uses our mouth again and again, till, someday, the mantra becomes our breathing, because the deepest layers of our being are impregnated by our prayer. This is a marvelous way of praying when we are tired.

It can also be helped by rhythms offered by life: our breathing in and out, the pace of our walking, etc. Many travelers have prayed this way with the rhythmical noise of the wheels of a train on the railroad. This is the method of religious songs, whose refrains tend to be short and easy to remember, as, for instance, in many Taizé hymns. It is the principle of singing the antiphon of the psalms for monks. It is the root of the method called *Centering Prayer.* Concerning this, I noticed a possible problem. A retreatant was praying with the word *Love,* and nothing was happening. Everything changed when we understood that she was praying with an intellectual concept, and when she took instead the phrase "God is Love" in John (1 Jn 4:8). The reference to the God of Jesus made a difference, and confirmed my instinct to invite people to pray with Scriptures.

For Our Children

I don't have too much to say, for any sort of verbal prayer, recited or sung, can be treated as a mantra. It is interesting to make children realize that one of their habits (and an aggravating one it is!) of repeating the same joke, the same question, the same mockery, the same silly song, or whatever, can be prayer. It is probably possible to use the "rap" style of singing, as well.

Silence

I mentioned meditation first because it is often called "the prayer of beginners." This expression is not a judgment on those who meditate. *No method says anything about our closeness to God* (neither does any spectacular spiritual gift!). Someone might be close to God without knowing any specific method of prayer, and a "master" in the ways of praying might not be. Indeed, who knows? We must abandon once and for all any judgment on this matter to God, as Paul did about himself: "But with me it is a very small thing that I should be judged by you or by any human court. I do not even judge myself. . . . It is the Lord who judges me" (1 Cor 4:3–4). The expression means only that meditation is easy, because our intellect can always use something to exercise it. Therefore, meditation can be practiced by people who are just embarking on a systematized prayer life. It is also common for beginners to be afraid of methods requiring greater passivity, because it is not easy to try to do "nothing" while praying. Eventually, however, meditation tires us. It is then time to employ other methods that help us to enter into spiritual passivity. This does not mean that we do nothing, but that we act in a way that lets God work more deeply within ourselves. We saw that praying with a picture or a melody gives priority to God's Word and not to our own. It is like applying to prayer the words of John the Baptist: "He must increase, but I must decrease" (Jn 3:30).

However, each one of us has a peculiar sort of passivity. This man will be engrossed by one nourishing thought, that woman by an efficacious picture; this one will be captured by one calming sentence of the gospel and that one by the humming of one line of a song. Thus, our heart slowly sinks into what is usually called contemplative prayer, where silence prevails. We do less and less (even though we might make efforts at the beginning to learn to do nothing, and stay quiet), because we allow God to act more and more freely. Progressively, repose quiets everything within us.

This "still" passivity is freedom, for we are no longer utterly manipulated by our unconscious motivations like self-satisfaction, self-protection, self-preoccupation, etc. In our prayer, God and we are free. Our being says, like Mary, "Let it be with me according to your word" (Lk 1:38). In my book *Is God Deaf?* I suggest we start our prayer periods with silence. When we can, it saves time, for we hear more quickly what God has to say.

In our world, noise is king and calls us to live at the surface of our being. So it is important to help children to discover, without fear, their inner silence. Some children like stillness spontaneously, but some others are forced into it because they have no siblings, both their parents work outside the home, etc. Thus, let us progressively educate children about silence in order to confirm their innate tendency, or to make them like what they did not choose, or to discover what they are unaware of. Let us never scream at them, "Silence! You are in the house of God!" as I saw a priest do.

In the primary school, silence was one of our first goals, for everyone working there. We used many means to ensure silence. For example, we had a short silent moment at the beginning of *every* class, in order to calm down, to get the attention ready (and to pray in classes for religion). At first, we played background music the children enjoyed, but that was relatively quiet. Silence followed music. Day after day, the type of music became quieter (thus we were able to introduce the children to some classical music), till it disappeared. We saw the children enjoy silence. The proof was that in increasing numbers they chose to enter into the "oratory" we had set for silence. They could go there freely, during their spare time, and read, color books, rest, or whatever. The only rule was, "Please, stay by yourself silently." So it was no surprise when parents would say to us, after our liturgies, "Tell me how you can make sixty or ninety kids, all around eight years of age, enter and stay so easily in an impressive silence!"

On vacation, we can add other means: to listen to the noises of the night at home or outside ("Let us see who is going to identify more sounds?"), to recognize the songs of birds, and so forth. Games can help (to go from one place to another without being spotted by the others, who keep their eyes closed). It is a joy to see children (and ourselves) no longer scared by their inner silence. Joy, for God can talk more easily and clearly through the "gentle breeze" that touched Elijah's heart, can call us by name like Samuel in the stillness of the night (1 Kings 19:12; 1 Sam 3:1–10): Is it not "while gentle silence enveloped all things, and night in its swift course was now half gone" that God's Word was heard? (Wis 18:14–15).

Chapter 7

How Can I Decode What Is Going On in My Prayer?

THE QUESTION might as well have been, "Why have I never heard God?" Most of the people who asked me this question talked in such a way that I had the impression they had expected to hear, physically, a voice coming from elsewhere. And also, they often compared themselves to individuals who claimed that they had heard God. After all, Paul says three times that he heard, on the road to Damascus, a voice say to him, "Saul, Saul, why do you persecute me?" (Acts 9; 22; 26). However, he does not specify where that voice came from. Other seekers have explained to me that they "heard" within themselves a voice other than their own. For instance, a friend of mine, in the last prayer period of a retreat, heard a voice starting by itself the Lord's Prayer within her, and a man heard clearly "I am" while he was still a nonbeliever, and that experience changed his life. Most of the people I'm thinking of here seemed to me psychologically healthy, so I accept their version of their experience (I must admit my skepticism about someone who claimed he had heard demonic voices but refused to record them the next time, although he did record our conversation). For who are we to decide how God is going to talk to anyone? However, I take seriously the cautions of most psychologists concerning such matters, and my experience has shown me that God usually speaks through simpler ways. Let us learn the ordinary means of God's communication with us, rather than yearn for something spectacular that may never happen. My book *Discernment* explains at length how to decode what is going on within ourselves when we want to make a decision with God. I describe the signals we get in prayer and how to decipher them. I'll summarize them here, applying them directly to prayer, aside from the use of discernment in making a decision. When we pray, we may experience *consolation or desolation,* classical terms that I often translate as *enlivening or stifling feelings.*

Consolation

There is consolation when the text we pray with creates within us enlivening feelings *at the deepest level of ourselves.* Peace, joy, hope, certainty, strength, and courage, for instance. These feelings are a signal: What is in tune with the life of Love within us has reacted; the Spirit and our spirit exult together within us because the text fits them both. Therefore, what the text describes or signifies, or the thoughts evoked by it within ourselves, are probably according to God's Spirit. So it is good to stay with that in order to cultivate it or to let it work by itself. The meaning of such an experience will become clear someday, for it might take time (see "Stay With It" in Chapter 3, "Why Doesn't Scripture Talk to Me?"). It is often helpful to talk about that with a good spiritual helper. This experience is not strange, for it is similar to what we feel when we look at a painting, listen to a piece of music, read a book, or talk with someone. We are touched by the contrast between colors, the bass that backs the musical theme, the description of the atmosphere of the scene, or one remark that was made to us. We are enlivened on the spot, whether we understand why or not.

Sometimes what we feel strikes us less than a new understanding of something concerning our faith or our life. It sounds almost intellectual, for it is a kind of knowledge, but it comes without the usual long process of any intellectual reasoning. It is like an unexpected and sudden light, an instantaneous intuition about something not so clearly perceived before: All of a sudden, we grasp the relationship between the colored surfaces of a painting, the significance of the chords regarding the melody, or the "why" of a specific phrase in a chapter of a book. Frequently, it is difficult for us to explain what we have caught in the twinkling of an eye. But, as an example, we have understood the freedom of Mary saying yes to the angel, and that she could not say no; or we have perceived Elizabeth's feeling when she greeted Mary: "As soon as I heard the sound of your greeting, the child in my womb leaped for joy" (Lk 1:38, 44). This consolation is called by the scholars *intellectual consolation*.

Desolation

On the other hand, a text sometimes creates in us stifling feelings, desolation. Trouble, sadness, doubt, hopelessness, paralysis, confusion, etc. This is the sign that the text has touched within us something that is unhealthy for us right now because it has some connection with our deadly tendencies. Spiritual authors would say that the Evil One is tempting us, and that our being reacts. This phenomenon may even happen with Scripture, as it did with Jesus when he was tempted by the Adversary in the desert (Mt 4:1–11). And it has happened many times since, when people have been deceived by gurus using the Bible for their own self-interest.

We guess then that it is detrimental for us to stay with texts giving us desolation. It is like remaining in the poisoned atmosphere of a movie, of a book, or of a conversation that would trigger the worst inclinations within us. At this specific moment of our life, better for us to leave such a text, which can damage our being and lead us to hurtful actions. Desolation is like a warning signal that we must seriously take into account.

Three Levels of Feelings

While talking about our emotions above, I underlined the phrase *at the deepest level of our feelings*. I must go back to this point, but I will just summarize, and complete if necessary, what I say in my book *Discernment* (pp. 35–55). We all know something like three levels of feelings within ourselves.

To be touched at *the core of ourselves* is a rare experience in our life; it happens once, twice, or never. When we read the New Testament (concerning Jesus or Paul, for instance) and the best mystical authors, we see that this is true. I emphasize this because some people claim that this occurs for them every Tuesday evening! This experience happens with total certainty, even though this certitude needs time to impregnate the whole of our daily life. December 25, 1886, in Notre Dame Cathedral in Paris, the French poet Paul Claudel (1868–1955) suddenly believed, but it took years for him to answer all his questions. Max Jacob, a French artist (1876–1944), believed when he saw a yellow Christ on a wall of his apartment; but for years, he kept going to Parisian prostitutes and begging God's pardon, before he changed his behavior and asked for baptism. Faith might be there, but the intellectual assent or the ethical conduct might need years to be accomplished by the slow impregnation of what happened one day at the core of the being.

We all experience *the most superficial level of feelings*. There, emotions follow each other rapidly, like endless ups and downs, like waves on the surface of the sea, as soon as a wind blows. It is you, me, but it is not the deepest reality of ourselves. The problem is not to remain trapped in that superficial level, which is so promoted by our society with the hammering announcement of sales every week or by the empty promises of political campaigns.

If we don't want to become like Yo-Yos, victims of the manipulations of our environment, it is important to spot, identify, and stay with the feelings we experience in *the median level* of ourselves. There the feelings last and are not easily disturbed, and therefore are not too many during a goodly length of time. Only the emotions we know at such a level allow us to decode what God is saying to us.

It is not unusual to experience, at the same time, the last two levels of feelings I have mentioned. For instance, when my mother died, I was sad, but at a deeper level of emotions I knew joy and gratitude for the kind of life that had been hers. A toothache, a worry, the premenstrual syndrome, can affect us without destroying our deep peace. Though we have all experienced the difference between the two levels, the superficial and the median one, we have not learned to apply such knowledge to our prayer life, where it is the key to decoding.

Decoding

To hear God is to be attentive to what is happening within ourselves, intellect, feelings, and body, while we are praying and, later, to decode it. A nonbeliever would say, "While I was looking at this painting, listening to that music, reading this text, I felt glad and peaceful." A believer, talking about the same situation, would say, "I was reading this text, and God gave me gladness and peace." Each one of us interprets the same inner events according to the traditions of his/her religious faith or no-faith. I can now summarize the most fundamental and basic rule of discernment in prayer, in a simple way, according to the Christian spiritual authors:

> I experience consolation = I listen, for God is talking.
> I experience desolation = I don't listen, for the Liar is talking.

Sometimes We Have to Refine Our Decoding

Sometimes we must refine the advice given above. Spiritual masters have always said that the Liar can give *apparent consolations,* and the Lord can give *apparent desolations.*

Some people, for conscious or subconscious reasons, really like what gives stifling feelings. For instance, sadomasochists find pleasure (so it is an apparent consolation) in what is morbid, and this might happen to us. For instance, the text we are praying with seems to give us enlivening feelings (in this case I prefer to say "enjoyable" feelings). However, the longer we stay with it, the worse the feelings. The fruit not being good, the tree certainly was not good either! (Mt 7:17–18). What was an apparent consolation leads in fact to desolation. I was delighted with David when "he saw a woman bathing, who was very beautiful." The longer I stayed with the text, the more ashamed I became; I understood the way I had been looking at my secretary (2 Sam 11:2). So, we had better not stay with such a text, its meaning, its imagery, or the thoughts it creates within us. Right now, it is not good for us, for it will just reinforce something that can become deadly within us.

Other times, the text with which we pray gives us, at first, feelings that seem stifling, like a desolation. However, we feel the certainty, though the "vibrations" we get are unpleasant, that we have to face what the text says to us. If what is happening is healthy, slowly we pass through what we had to confront. It is an apparent desolation because it is a kind of death through which we must pass in order to know new life. It is a Passover for a kind of resurrection and, if managed well, it ends in consolation. When Jesus said to me, "How hard it is for the rich to enter the kingdom of God!" I felt bad, but I could not leave the sentence. Later, I discovered that I had worshiped my reputation like an idol, and that I had to let that go (Mk 10:23). So, understandably, the beginning is not likable, and that explains the apparent stifling feelings (in this case, I prefer to say "difficult" feelings). And it is true that in this situation, we don't usually suffocate, as we do in real desolation; we just breathe with greater difficulty.

It is possible now to summarize what our behavior must be when we experience an apparent consolation or desolation ("enjoyable" or "difficult" feelings, in the median level of feelings).

- Apparent Consolation = I listen with great caution, for it is not God who is talking, it is probably the Liar, and I won't accept what I have heard.

- Apparent Desolation = I listen carefully, for it seems that the Liar is talking, but it is probably God who wants me to face something difficult, which is eventually going to be good for me.

The reader has understood that, in these circumstances, it is necessary to allow time for what is going on to unfold, and that it is good to be helped by a qualified spiritual helper. But the more experienced we become about decoding our own prayer life, the easier it will be for us to distinguish apparent and real consolations or desolations.

My Psyche or God?

After these explanations, some readers will ask, "So, then, when I am praying, am I not just talking to myself?" Some psychologists think the same. What can we say? I was a Jesuit student in philosophy when I went to one of my teachers with the same question. Here are the outlines of our dialogue. The teacher: "Do you believe that God is a pure spirit?" I: "I do." He: "Do you believe that we human beings are a mixture of matter and spirit?" I: "I do." He: "If it is so, any word of God to us exists for us and reaches us only through our being, matter and spirit. God *cannot talk* to our spirit without passing through the mixture we are. If God could use another way, we would not hear anything. That is the way we hear God, and we have no other way." Therefore, any action of God within us is always something *of* us, of our body, of our intellect, or of our emotions.

It is interesting to notice that the ones yearning for a vision or a word still depend on seeing or hearing. God cannot communicate without passing through our body and psyche. The question is, therefore, to know how to decode the signals we perceive there according to the traditions of our faith.

With the explanations given here, we will be able to decode what we have experienced in our prayer periods. We must go back to what has given us consolation (enlivening feelings, sometimes after difficult feelings): the text and its meaning, the images and thoughts produced by it. Through that, we'll discover more and more clearly the message of God's Spirit. Similarly, through what has provoked desolation (stifling feelings, sometimes after enjoyable feelings), we'll see more and more easily what the Father of Lies tried to suggest to us. It is obvious that decoding requires time (see Chapter 8, "Do I Have to Keep a Journal?").

For Our Children

Is decoding too complicated for children? It is not, if we teach them a minimum of it, and I have done it.

I remember my conversations with a well-balanced ten-year-old Alsatian. I said to him things like these: "Give attention to what you may feel. Not on the surface but deep, deep down within yourself. And when and if you see that you have always felt good about something, probably you can follow your idea. On the contrary, the longer you think about something, check out if you feel worse and worse. In that case, forget it, for it may not be good for you right now. In any case, take your time." He became able to decode the meaning of most of his inner experiences, to find the value of time and to discover his inner world systematically.

This kind of training is more difficult when we work with teenagers. The transformations they are undergoing in their bodies provoke disturbances in their feelings, and it is not easy for them to perceive at what level they are emotionally affected (as a matter of fact, I found a similar problem with women experiencing difficult menopauses). But that was for me one more reason to try to teach them the content of this chapter. For it is when we pass through uneasy times that we most need to decode what is going on within ourselves. I can testify that it is possible and useful and effective to give teenagers the advice elaborated on here, because I have done that for years with many male and female teenagers, in the classroom, in spiritual accompaniment, and in directed retreats. Not too long ago, I met one of my former students, and she acknowledged that our conversations on this kind of subject in our classroom had been very helpful in the conduct of her first romantic relationship.

Chapter 8

Do I Have to Keep a Journal?

THE ANSWER for this question depends on where we are in our spiritual journey and on what we want to achieve. I am in a crisis, and I want some light in order to get out of it; I have to make an important decision; I would like to deepen more systematically what has touched me powerfully; I desire to answer more faithfully to God; I feel within myself something that wants to be born or to be developed, etc. All these experiences invite me to pray in such a way that I can get more clearly the information I need. The preceding chapters have given advice for this purpose and explained how to decode what might happen in our prayer. But we must also gather methodically what we have to decode, because many days may pass before we hear God's final word on the subject. If we have not put down and kept some written notes, we won't remember everything. As we keep a journal during a trip, so might we with our prayer periods. It is the best means to help our memory.

A Few Notes

To keep a journal does not require volumes of memoirs and does not mean we expatiate about ourselves through pages in a narcissistic self-contemplation. We need merely jot down on paper a few notes about what happened to us during our prayer time. We allow five minutes for this after we have finished praying. The notes we take are not a second meditation about what occurred while we were praying, and they concern three things.

1. *What* has touched me.

   We just mention the references of the text we prayed with. It is good to copy the verse that has been the most powerful for us (when we reread our notes, it will be there in black on white, and in the translation of the Bible we have used while praying). For example, Isa 43:1–5, especially verse 4: "You are precious in my sight... and I love you." If we have been touched by the whole story, we write down what has affected us the most. For instance, Jn 11:1–44, "all that account of Lazarus' death."

2. *How* (much) I was touched.

   Here we write down the feelings we have experienced. This is the most important, for it says if we knew consolation or desolation, the basics for discernment, signals given to our heart. A few words are enough: "Peace, Joy," or "Sadness, Depression," for instance. It is important to specify the intensity of the feelings. Because, as I have explained in Chapter 3, "Why Doesn't Scripture Talk to Me?," a strong emotion invites us to go back to the same text, and a feeling that is just "nice" tells us to take another text. So, for example, "Increasing strong Peace and Joy," or, "Sudden powerful sadness and depression."

3. *Why* I was touched by this text.

   When we experience very strong feelings, very often we are not conscious of any thought in our mind. We are all joy or tears, without knowing why! Our third point is empty, proving the strength of our emotions. But usually while we are praying, some thoughts are in our mind (the advice here is, "Let them come, let them go," without trying to elaborate on them too much). Ordinarily, these thoughts explain why we are touched by the spe-

cific text used in our prayer. It is with these thoughts that
our intellect will be able to do its business, chiefly when
we decode what happened to us. Though priority is given
to the heart in our prayer, the mind does not go to sleep.
It waits and will be exercised fully afterward, when we
evaluate the fruit of our prayer periods. In 1 Corinthians
14, Paul does not renounce the intellect for discerning the
value of all charisms.

Putting together 1, 2, and 3 above, we might already
"hear" something at the moment we write down our notes.
For instance, "While praying with [1] 'For you are precious
in my eyes, and I love you,' I felt [2] an increasing joy, because, [3] for the first time I understood how much I am
unique and precious for God; because, usually, my self-image
is not good." Or, another example, "While praying [1] with
the story of Lazarus' death, [2] I was suddenly grasped by
a deeper and deeper sadness, because, [3] my father's death
came back to my mind, and I realized that I had never taken
time to grieve." It is easy to see where, spiritually, one is who
prayed thus. The same method can be applied when we pray
about the events of our life. It is explained in Chapter 10,
"Can I Pray With the News?"

The two examples above would not exactly require a journal, because the information is given in one single prayer
period. But usually each prayer period gives simply part of
the information we need. It is only after days of formal
prayer that the message appears more and more clearly, and
more easily if we are used to discernment and/or helped by a
qualified spiritual helper. Between the first impact and the total discovery of God's message, we might spend days, weeks,
or months. At the time of evaluation, our journal allows
us to reread the whole process, which our memory cannot
remember in all its details.

The reader has guessed that a journal is of great value
for the meetings with our spiritual helper. With our notes at
hand (and a summary we have prepared), it is easier for us

to explain what happened in our prayer, and for the spiritual helper to understand our journey.

To Be Able to Close the Book

It seems to me that someday we must stop writing a journal, except for times of crisis, of retreat, and of discernment for an important decision. To keep a journal is still to look at ourselves. The Evil One knows how to use any reason, even the best one, to keep us in our self-centeredness: to become more faithful, to stay vigilant, to know where I am in my journey, etc. If we stay too long writing about ourselves, we may forget that God and our neighbor must be the sole center of our attention. A journal is a noble ambition that can become a subtle refusal to give ourselves up and give God absolute priority. We can close our notebook, chiefly when we have learned enough about ourselves and our God, enough about discernment. If our spiritual sensitivity has been sufficiently refined, we have acquired the knowledge and reflexes that will work easily in all circumstances of our life: Soon enough, we'll be able to discover the information we need and to decode it, and to know where we are and where our God is.

When do we close our notebook? It depends on each one of us, of course. Most of the people I have helped spiritually on a regular basis have kept a systematic daily journal no longer than five years.

For Our Children

Very young children cannot write, but we can invite them to keep the drawings they have made about religious subjects (or we can do that, and date them and record the circumstances). Children *and* adults experience a special joy when they see, later, their past work. I remember my nephews in front of their first "letters" to me; I keep the drawings of my little neighbors for some later day. To go back to such things is to reread one's past. And if the subject was religious, we get in touch with the person we were spiritually at that time, and the Being who was our God. Sometimes it is striking to see that the God of our youth was saying already what we still hear today in prayer or daily life!

We can employ the idea of a journal for children who write easily, but only for the end of a day of retreat, for instance. We can then invite them to write down the discoveries they have made about themselves, the world, Jesus, and God. They can illustrate by a drawing what has been particularly powerful for them and touched their heart, in order to go back to that later. Drawing helps them to become aware of their own spiritual "portrait" and/or of "their" God at that specific moment of their life. They may be motivated to develop for a while, more systematically, a new relationship with Jesus (as a shepherd, as a child, etc.) or with God (as a Father, as a listener, etc.). For some young teenagers, going on retreat before their Confirmation, this has been a fruitful experience. With older teenagers, keeping a journal for a while may be helpful, for such personal writing might also prove cathartic. *The Diary of Anne Frank,* although tragic, remains the best example of that.

Chapter 9

Do I Have to Prepare
My Prayer Times?

THE QUESTION could have been, "Do we prepare ourselves appropriately to meet our Beloved?" Watch a
teenager who is going to meet his sweetheart: In front
of a mirror, he checks out the way his hair is combed, the
look of his clothes, and, if you could see his brain and heart,
you would perceive the first very excited and the second full
of emotions! More subtly, when we have invited friends for
supper, we prepare the living room and the table, we put on
casual or dressy clothes, we think about what we are going to share, and as we make these preparations, our heart
is already singing. At least, this is what happens if we take
the time. Why not do the same for our Guest "par excel-
lence"? Our preparation reveals the value we confer on the
encounter.

When people enter religious life, they learn how to pray. A
part of that training is to prepare their prayer. Usually, they
prepare in the evening, before going to bed, what they are
going to pray with the next morning. We can all benefit from
this old and wise custom.

Preparing Holistically

Preparing Our Body

To prepare our body is, first, to be sure that we are not exhausted when we start to pray. A tired body cannot pray. I used to recommend to people who were going to make a thirty-day retreat with me that they arrive at the retreat house very rested. To prepare the body is also to remember the bodily postures that have been the most helpful for us recently, in order to take one of them when we start to pray. Finally, we can prepare some of the other means I mention in Chapter 4, "While I Pray, What Do I Do With My Body?"

Preparing Our Mind

Above all, this part of the preparation consists of selecting the text we'll pray with (see Chapter 3, "Why Doesn't Scripture Talk to Me?"). Then we can look at the text more closely to be aware of what strikes us the most, and what first thoughts come to mind. It is the time to look for extra information about the text, to read the footnotes or introductory remarks in our Bible, to consult the commentary of a scholar or a Father of the Church. This allows us to nourish our mind before praying and to satisfy our intellectual curiosity. Everything our mind might need during the prayer period will have been prepared before praying, and thus we won't overload our moment with God with unnecessary baggage. We know and prepare all the ingredients of the recipe we are going to cook and enjoy the next day! One benefit of this is that if we have read solid explanations of the text, we are not going to make Scriptures say things they never meant. For example, we have verified that the first two parables of Luke 15 are centered on the joy of the shepherd or the woman who has found what was lost, sheep or coin. At the moment of praying with Luke 15:11–32, we'll know that the third parable is not about the so-called "Prodigal Son," but about the father, joyful and prodigal in his forgiveness and love. So we might be more focused on God's prodigality in the sense of magnanimity toward us than on our sins. During the preparation, it is helpful to jot down some brief notes to keep in front of us when we pray.

Another preparation exists that is a more ongoing process than what I have just described. It is traditionally known as "spiritual reading." The masters in spirituality can give us a lot, and it is good to know their works, because everything they say has been the fruit of their own prayer. Our spiritual helper can guide us to find the authors whose writings will be appropriate for the person we are, at this specific leg of our journey with God. Although this is part of our mental preparation, it is also a stage in the preparation of the heart.

Preparing Our Heart

To prepare our heart means merely to desire the encounter, to enter into it with trust and generosity. It is easy to say, but not always easy to do. Sometimes, like moody children sullenly eating a dish they usually relish, we pray grudgingly. Or we greet with boredom God's word, or even God. Other times, somewhere within ourselves, all of "that" does not seem to interest us, although we know that we need it. There is a long list of circumstances that prevent us from praying with a joyful heart. Because this book is chiefly about methods and tools, I won't discuss these feelings and their causes. I'll just say here, that at the deepest level of ourselves, beyond our immediate feelings, let us verify if we really want to go to God. If our answer is yes, let us go. If it is no, we should clarify the situation with our spiritual helper (concerning such a disposition, reading the classics in spirituality might already give us some answers).

I want to go back to something that seems like just a detail, the fact that spiritual authors recommend that we prepare our prayer period before going to bed. When we do so, we give our being matter to ruminate about all night long, and I believe that our heart prays with our preparation while we sleep. Many people who have practiced this method have been happily surprised by what happened the following morning. This reminds us of artists who, for a long time, carried within themselves the project of a painting, sculpture, piece of music, book, and eventually saw it coming out beautifully. It is like a pregnant woman who finally delivers the baby that her whole being had prepared for nine months.

When we invite friends for supper and don't have too much time to prepare the meal, we cook simple dishes that can be made quickly. However, our heart is present. Similarly, when we don't have time for our usual preparation, let us use the first minutes of our prayer period for that (this reinforces the importance of taking enough time to pray). What is ultimately essential is to desire the encounter with all our heart. But we know that chefs are so talented that they can make a delicious meal in a few minutes. If we have prepared our prayer for months, we'll be able to do it successfully in a short time. Also, according to the principle explained in Chapter 3, "Why Doesn't Scripture Talk to Me?," if a text has been powerful for us, we have just "to stay with it." Therefore, no preparation is necessary.

For Our Children

As parents and educators, we give advance preparation to our children's prayer life through everything they learn about God and Jesus, and about our own relationship with Jesus and his God. It is also everything they see us living out. If our children have savored forgiveness, prayer about it is easy; if they saw us admiring God's loving work in a marvelous sunset or a wonderful sculpture or a great act of mercy reported by the news, praise won't be difficult for them.

The other kind of preparation must be really close to the moment of prayer. In the primary school, we prepared the children in many ways. We would give them all the technical information just before praying, in order not to disturb them during the prayer time itself ("We'll start with a song, then we'll hear a story. We'll all stay silent for a very short while. Finally, Mrs. So-and-So will lead the last song." Or, "A short story said by Jesus will be read to us. Then we'll be given some questions about it. Then we'll all reflect silently about the questions for a few seconds. Finally, Mr. So-and-So will help us to share our thoughts."). However, we were careful not to say everything in advance, in order to surprise and delight the children during the prayer time (for instance, it is only during our liturgy about Christmas that the children would see the whole Nativity scene made on a board, with the different characters they had prepared days before our celebration). Then we would invite the children to check out the distance between themselves and their neighbors, to take a comfortable body posture, and to enter into "a few seconds" of silence as a final preparation. This has always worked well. We never had to reprimand someone's behavior (at most, one of us would have to move a child away from his/her neighbor, gently and silently, when we noticed that the proximity was creating a problem).

And we would repeat again and again to the oldest ones, "See, you can do the same, when you want to pray to Jesus by yourselves" (as a matter of fact, I used the same method with prisoners for retreats in correctional facilities, and I know that some inmates practiced what they had learned when they were by themselves in their cells). As for teenagers, they can prepare their prayer times as adults do.

Chapter 10

Can I Pray With the News?

I COULD ABSTAIN from answering the question by referring the reader to the Old Testament. For Jews and Christians, God speaks through the stories found in it. Most of them concern political situations (to a lesser degree, the New Testament does the same). I used the word *political* according to its Greek root: *politikos* means everything about the life of the city, the *polis*. So God speaks through any political event. And because we are asked to pray with these words of God, I can assert, "no politics without prayer, no prayer without politics." Since the news is connected, one way or another, to politics, I have to explain how politics is part of an authentic prayer life.

No Politics Without Prayer

The life of a city results from all relationships existing between the families it comprises. By enlarging this notion to the network that makes a nation, to all the countries dealing with one another, we have the current word *politics*. And it is through the news that we are aware about politics.

The life of a "city" depends on the decisions made at any level, and our status as citizens invites us to be a part of it. If we want to act in a responsible way, individually or together, we need to discern. It is also in our best interest, for any governmental decision affects us: Foreign policy guarantees or not our security and peace; financial choices increase or decrease our taxes; the medical policy assures or not that we are going to be given health care; decisions of justice take care or not of our rights, etc. Being Christian adds something: To let God-Love act through us leads us to serve all our neighbors, and our neighborhood is as wide as the world. So, at our level of responsibility and power, we must make our choices according to and with God, through a discernment that requires prayer about news. My book *Discernment* deals systematically with the decision-making process; here, I will simply emphasize what more specifically concerns prayer life.

Every choice requires *lucidity* and *honesty*, and, for us Christians, according to Jesus' message about God. Lucidity implies, of course, that we study seriously the object of a choice, as related by the news: What is possible here and now, the value of a program or a candidate, the impact on all of a proposed law, etc. For this task, nonbelievers go back within themselves to the deepest values they believe in. But for Christians, this is not done only according to current values but according to evangelical criteria, like priority given to the poor or care for the outcast. Lucidity means also that we clarify our motivations for choosing, in order not to be swayed merely by money, power, and glory, as so much of the public is. For a Christian, such clarification is done not only because of a value system, but essentially in the face of the message and the person of Jesus Christ.

This lucidity is fruitful if we can be honest before God, ourselves, and others, beyond what the news says. But this is possible only if we go back unceasingly to the One we cherish the most, the One we house, God; and this is done *in prayer.* There, we let the One we love purify our convictions and intentions, correct our ways of looking at people and things; we let Jesus teach us how to serve as he did; we allow the Spirit of Love to take over and rule our behaviors. There, I hope, we can be honest (if not, we had better pray for God's mercy!).

In the core of ourselves, prayer also gives *courage.* For we need courage to stand up to powerful people, interest groups, political parties or unions, electors, media, according to what we have heard or seen. We face the same situations with our parents or in-laws, our relatives or friends, neighbors or co-workers. Where can we find courage, if not in God, *through prayer?* There, we are refilled with the life of Love, with the sap of the Vine, with the Breath; there, we bind ourselves again with the One who said to Ezekiel, "Stand up," and who made him do so (Ezek 2). There, we receive once more the grace to be disciples and servants, for the sake of the world.

People who follow the news at all levels, and want to be part of the life of the "city," need a deep prayer life. It is possible: I have worked for years with individuals whose milieu, the economic field, is as tough as the political one. And these were people who prayed and acted according to what they discerned as God's message in prayer. French people of my age remember Edmond Michelet, former attorney general of France, who was praised by all when he died (it was not the kind of eulogy we hear at some funerals with embarrassment, because it does not sound true with a lot of superlatives and comparatives). This man had been, according to everyone, an uncommon witness of Christ *in* politics. I end by imitating the old pastor of the parish of my youth. He used to say, "Democracy is a political regime for saints." Therefore, it is for people who pray. If we don't find God in prayer, we won't find God in life. I can now assert truthfully, "No healthy politics, for ourselves and others, without an authentic prayer life." All of this might seem obvious to anyone who wants to be faithful to Jesus, his message, and his God. Is it also obvious to say, "No prayer without politics"?

No Prayer Without Politics

Jesus said, "Every good tree bears good fruit" and "Not everyone who says to me, 'Lord, Lord,' will enter the kingdom of heaven, but only the one who does the will of my

Father in heaven" (Mt 7:17, 21). So he strongly says to us that any recourse to his name is effective only if we act according to his Father's will, which is, "You shall love the Lord your God . . . and your neighbor as yourself" (Lk 10:27). We know that to love in the New Testament means, first of all, to serve. So we cannot imagine prayer without action for others, and particularly for the sake of the neediest ones (Mt 25:31–46). And the news gives us enough information about the needy people all around us, whom we can serve.

The irrefutable message of Jesus is confirmed by what happened to those who were in contact with him. Zacchaeus is a good example of that: He was curious, just "trying to see what Jesus was like." But as soon as Jesus was in his home, he changed his policy. "Half of my possessions, Lord, I will give to the poor; and if I have defrauded anyone of anything, I will pay back four times as much" (Lk 19:8). I could also mention the Samaritan woman, Mary of Magdala, the disciples, the Twelve. Meeting Jesus transformed them, and changed their influence on their environment, "even to the ends of the earth" (Jn 4; 20:18; Acts 1:8). Anybody aware about history knows that the testimony of the first Christians finally had an enormous political impact on Europe.

To encounter God through Jesus, to give their Spirit of Love the freedom to work within us, *cannot not have a political outcome,* in our city, nation, and the ends of the earth. If our prayer does not give such a result, we must doubt its authenticity. For instance, prayer is enjoyed by some spiritual "schizophrenics." These are people who trap themselves in a so-called spiritual world that is not in this world, which is the only place where we can meet God. If we don't find God in life, we won't find God in prayer. Jews and Christians believe in a God we deal with in history and who always sends us back to history. It is even more obvious for Christians, for whom God became part of our human condition in Jesus. That is why a true intimate encounter with this God creates, sooner or later, a change in the one who prays that affects his/her environment. The political fruit of prayer proves its authenticity. Here again, I can now assert, "No true prayer without impact on politics."

Praying With the News

To be aware of the life of the "city" requires us to get news concerning it. Then the question becomes, "How to pray with the news?" Of course, it depends on each one of us: our own nature, our spiritual and emotional condition, our usual interests, our responsibilities, our education, and so forth. Despite these individual differences, it is possible to indicate some ways that will work for most of us.

First, we must inform ourselves as well as possible. Some people would say ironically, "Ah, because you believe in the news? Do you remember an ambush in Afghanistan, a massacre in Romania during the fall of the communist regime, a tank of a truck caught on fire, for instance, that were faked by some TV channels?" It has always been more or less like that, going back to the first gazettes and town criers. The people publishing the news, or the people behind them, have always had their own ideas and interests about the narrated events. If we compare 1 and 2 Kings to 1 and 2 Chronicles, we see that the writers did not share the same perspectives, or the same prejudices, concerning the same events. Even the four gospels show different emphases about the same revelation. So, the accuracy of the news has traditionally depended on the objectivity of whoever transmitted it. Therefore let us do what we can to inform ourselves as exactly as possible about the life of the "city," the politics. Using several types of media, completing what we know with experts' comments, learning how to read between the lines, etc. help us to get a better knowledge of what is related by the news. Many means exist to learn how to become well-informed.

Moreover, we bring our awareness about the "city" into our encounter with God, during which we can experience a challenge and a call, repentance and purification, intercession and thanksgiving, and contemplation.

While I am writing, war is still going on in Bosnia-Herzegovina and Rwanda; South Africa lives its first year without apartheid; Amnesty International includes in its goals the defense of people persecuted because of their sexual orientation. I could also make a list of more local news: A woman saves a young boy who was drowning, a fight between two gangs ends in the death of a teenager, etc. All of this creates *a challenge and a call,* e.g., what do we do for these people while attending meetings for the coming elections; where do we stand in terms of racism; how do we behave in front of the persecuted ones around us? If necessary, the news might invite us to *repentance* and *purification;* we ask God's forgiveness for our indifference or our prejudices. When we cannot do anything directly about the situation, we can still intercede for the victims and the perpetrators (I speak abundantly of *intercession* in my book *God's Passion, Our Passion*). Finally, good news may inspire *thanksgiving:* for those working tirelessly for peace or against discrimination, for God's grace in them and in me if I act like them. Thus, exactly as we read, ponder, and pray the Bible with seriousness, so we can read, ponder, and pray the news, and check out the consistency of our behavior with our faith. Through it, we hear the news God has for us today, according to the Good News of Jesus Christ.

But praying with the news goes even further. It gives us the opportunity to *contemplate* God's mystery in human history, as the Jews did all through the Old Testament. We see the mystery of God-Love suffering in those who are robbed or calumniated, beaten or killed, forgotten or raped, and also in those committing those crimes. We behold the mystery of God-Love patient and tenacious, struggling and hoping, giving and given up in all the people who serve with fidelity; the mystery of God living all of that in believers and non-believers, and in ourselves. Such a contemplation says more about Jesus' God than any sunset or chain of mountains, because this God is never so visible as in human beings. That is why praying with the news can impregnate us to the point of changing us.

Eventually, praying this way gives us graces that belong to contemplative prayer, like the prayer of the monks who, since the fourth century, have seemed out of the world (although their "political" impact on history cannot be denied). "Wasting" our time for God's mystery in the world becomes a grace of *distance* and *gratuity*. Distance allows us to put each piece of news in its rightful place, not confusing the concern for a skater, a singer, or a football hero with the worries for millions of refugees, for example; through that we better know where we are called to act. And last but not least, to leave our usual business and pray with the news of God's mystery teaches us gratuity: Seemingly we do nothing effective but pray. But this reminds us that people are not useless because they are not producing something. Think, for instance, of children who are not yet working, the elderly and invalids who lack mobility, poets and artists who speak about things other than production. They can all still love. So do we, because praying with the news might become time spent not for ourselves but for others before the Other, the Transcendent Love present in all human beings. At that level, prayer joins the arts.

For Our Children

The news gives many possibilities to pray with children. We can use meditation and help them reflect on a specific event. We have just to be able to make the news of the world reach the children's own world: A war can be connected with their own conflicts in their family or with their friends; a program about South Africa without apartheid sends them back to their own prejudices in school; hearing about volunteers working in poor countries might invite them to care for a handicapped neighbor. Contemplation is looking at pictures, watching a videocassette, making drawings about a news item. Hearing songs of other cultures and dialoguing with foreigners about their country helps verbal prayer and intercession. And when the news is good, it is easy to give thanks.

This last point suggests two things to keep in mind when we pray about the news with children. First, we must maintain a balance between bad and good news. I think it's important to emphasize the enlivening items, without overlooking the terrible facts of human life. We don't have to put on children's shoulders the weight of our sins in the world; they will have plenty of time, later, to deal with them and their consequences. Also, better to help them admire God's Love in action in our midst, and thus to invite them to give freedom to the Spirit of Service wherever they are. We should tilt them toward positive role models, although we must avoid creating an idol with any "hero."

Finally, if some people would still question the value of praying with the news for children, I would reply, "It is good to train them early to become authentic citizens of their nation and of the world. But, chiefly, and this explains my emphasis on international examples, it is rather marvelous to prepare their hearts to embrace the world, to *be* a heart like God's."

NOTE: I did not include anything about "praying with our personal life," for two main reasons. First, it pertains to what I have said above, if we say that we pray with the "news" of our own life. So the content of this chapter can be applied to that kind of prayer. Also, it seems to me that we all spontaneously pray more easily with our personal events than with the events given us through the news. So I chose to emphasize what for most of us is less spontaneous, but not less important, for our personal world is always influenced by the whole world. "Enlarge the site of your tent," says God to us (Isa 54:2). Finally, since each person has a special way to pray with his/her life, I can make no generally applicable comment, except that we have to learn to hear what God says through the news of our own life.

For that purpose, we can use the questions of Chapter 8, "Do I Have to Keep a Journal?"

1. "*What* has touched me?" The point here is the event affecting us, through a letter, a problem in our neighborhood, the birth of a child, a funeral, etc. For example: I see a woman helping somebody to cross the street, and neither obviously belongs to the same ethnic group; my cousins divorce.

2. "*How* (much) I was touched." I just add that it is important here to verify if we were touched on the superficial level of feelings, by an event objectively important: This might mean that we are not or cannot be a part of a world wider than our own; and so we have to explain to ourselves why not. The same verification is necessary when we see ourselves deeply moved by an event that is not too big, for it might be significant for our inner being. Back to the examples: I was deeply lifted up, or, I was disturbed for days.

3. "*Why* I was touched by this text." It is with the answers to this question that our intellect will be able to work, to decode what happened to us. Slowly, by discerning, we hear what God says to us through the event. For instance: God confirms my desire to be less and less racist, or, God challenges my way of being a spouse. It is important to remember that sometimes it is better to confront the "Scripture" of our daily life than to pray with the Bible, in order not to escape what we must face (in fact, we won't be able to pray with a text, because the event will distract us. We are back to what I say in Chapter 13, "What Can I Do When I Am Distracted in Prayer?")

Through all of that, we understand that to discern is to decode, with the same method, *everything* that affects us deeply through a text, an event, or people. God speaks to us everywhere in our own history.

Chapter 11

Must I Pray About My Sins?

T HE LAST CHAPTER has evoked our deficiencies as Jesus' witnesses, and therefore our sins. But this book is about the concrete ways of praying, and not a treatise about prayer, so I won't say too much on the benefits of praying about our sins, particularly when our motivation is the desire to be forgiven. When we ask someone we have offended for forgiveness, we signify that we are attached to the relationship that has been hurt. We mean that the bond is precious for us (even, precisely, when we are still centered on *our* selfish fear of losing the other or on our need to get back *our* own inner peace, without giving priority to the other in our initiative). I won't dwell, either, on the humility included in our pleading for forgiveness.

Some people would answer the question "Must I pray about my sins?" with, "Of course, for we are sinners, and it is in Scripture!" It is not so obvious, and sometimes praying about our sins is not to be recommended on the ground that it can deepen depression or develop within us a devastating guilt complex. To insist too much on Jesus as our Redeemer might make us forget that his Spirit can lead *us* to act according to the gospel. Therefore, here again, discernment is beneficial, and sometimes necessary, for we often confuse ethical behavior with faith. Here is some information (see also Chapter 7, "How Can I Decode What Is Going On in My Prayer?").

When we pray about our sin or our sins (I'll explain later this distinction), we usually experience some *sadness*. The flavor of it will tell us if we must stay with such a prayer or not. If the sadness is a desolation, better to immediately stop praying about our sins; on the other hand, if it is a consolation, it is good to keep praying like that. We can name the bad sadness a *guilt complex,* and the good one *contrition.* How can we distinguish one from another?

Guilt Complex or Contrition

A guilt complex starts like a sadness but quickly becomes a deep depression. We judge and condemn ourselves unceasingly. The condemnation does not end with a clear verdict and punishment erasing the fault. On the contrary, we are caught in a vicious circle where we are simultaneously judge and criminal in *an endless trial.* It is a lasting torture fed by new charges or the unceasing return of the same one. "It is my fault. I should not have done it. If I had only acted otherwise. I could have . . . " This narcissistic and masochistic excruciation is not healthy, for it is exclusively and indefinitely centered on the most negative side of ourselves. Some signs confirm: We function rather badly in our family or at our work because we are trapped within ourselves; our world grows narrower, and we run away from others; we ignore what would make us encounter the Other, God — prayer, sacraments, and Scriptures. Often the phrases we use to describe our fault show that we are essentially turned toward the past. Or, if we evoke the future, it is without hope under the weight of what we did. So, better to stop praying about our sin when and if to do so only deepens our desolation.

Contrition is exactly the opposite. At first, it is a sadness, too. But its unfolding can even create a sort of joy. No question about it, contrition is also a trial, where, as the judge, we condemn the guilty sinner we are. But this trial comes to an end, and in the verdict is born a life force pushing us toward the one we have hurt, in order to ask for and to obtain forgiveness. Here, the tendency is more and more centered on the person we have offended. We leave ourselves and go back with a new energy to the other, and especially to God through prayer, sacraments, and Scripture. The process is full of hope and certainty: hope for forgiveness and reconciliation, and certainty that this is a new start for the wounded relationship. Contrition sees the future as a new chance, certain that everything is possible. It is a Passover within us that already believes in a Resurrection. And if we are sure of the other's love and forgiveness, our contrition is impregnated with joy. This is a consolation. So it is good to stay with what creates it, as long as it is fruitful. When forgiveness and reconciliation are complete, the past will exist only as a lesson and as an opportunity to give thanks, never for the sin itself, but for the grace that came out of it.

Paul confirms this description in 2 Corinthians 7. There, he rejoices for the sadness his former letter (which we don't have) provoked in the faithful of Corinth. Indeed, that "sorrow that came from God," "which stems from God," "led to repentance," and produced "holy zeal," and an "ardent desire to restore the balance of justice." And he distinguishes this "sorrow for God's sake [that] produces a repentance without regrets, leading to salvation" from a "worldly sorrow [that] brings death."

Patterns

When the risk of a morbid narcissism is removed, to pray about our sins is all gain, because we ask God not only for forgiveness, but also for strength not to repeat the sin if the same temptation returns. However, changing our behavior supposes that we pray in a way giving us information that helps us to achieve that goal. Instead of merely staying with the litany of our sins, we do better to discover *our usual patterns*.

So we must pray through seriously examining one of our specific sins. In what kind of circumstances does it happen?

Concerning what or whom? Questions like these help our discernment. For instance: "Do I sin in this peculiar way when I am too tired or too excited, when it is a question of my reputation or money, in front of an authority or someone disagreeing with me?" It is also important to see if this specific sin is an exception in our life, or symbolizes a tendency that repeats itself; a usual propensity reveals who we are more than an exception. Finally, it is useful to know how the process unfolds, from the temptation to the sinful act. How does it start? What is fueling it? Can I discern the different links of that chain of evil that ends with the sin? The more our knowledge of each of our sins increases, the greater our capacity to avoid it later.

Scripture is a marvelous assistance for this. The Bible is a huge panoply of male and female sinners who demonstrate for us the fundamental structures of all sins. And, as I say in Chapter 2, "What Is the Use of Praying With Scriptures?," generations of believers have refined the analysis of sins and of the sinner's behavior. So, to pray with their texts will facilitate and deepen our own discoveries. The companionship of our brother David or Peter, of our sister the wife of Job or the wife of Hosea, of Adam and Eve, will benefit us as we grapple with the sinful experiences of human beings since the beginning of history. But the last two names mentioned invite me to speak about praying about our *sin,* singular.

Our Sin: One of the Best Channels for "Our" Revelation

I prefer to speak about praying "about our *sin*" than "about our *sinfulness,*" for this last word clearly implies that we are "full" of sin without room for some good within ourselves. Understanding our sin helps us to acknowledge and own our permanent weakness, with a healthy realism and sense of responsibility. And it invites us to desire and to discover that we have a Savior. This is clear for every intelligent person.

Less obvious to many people is the following remark about the value of praying about our sin.

It seems that our sin is our only way to understand how much God wanted us to be *free*. We have been given such a freedom that we can even say no to God, to Love itself, in our heart and our behavior. A child or teenager says no to see if we give him/her the right to be free. We do the same with God through our sin. The infraction of the parental or social law, of the divine law, seems to be the only means to verify if we are free. And God accepts the test, respects our rebellion, as Jesus' Passion proves, tragically and marvelously. We repeat the refusal of God of all the characters of the Passion, and the sky does not fall on our heads, as it did not on their Good Friday evening. Reading daily in the newspapers the terrible list of the atrocities we commit against Love can become a sorrowful homage to God's immense respect for our freedom. Parents who have suffered from their children's deeds know that.

But if we understand this respect, we can also grasp something of the "unbelievable" Love it reveals. As children, we understood the love of our parents, chiefly the day we were scared to lose it because of our wrongdoing and got it back in totality through their forgiveness. In Adam and Eve, we did not believe that God-Love was ready to give us everything, and we chose to satisfy our covetousness by ourselves; thus, breaking our bond of love with God, we started a chain of evil and became the origin of a series of hurts through history, and we do the same now, every time we sin. We are Adams and Eves (Gen 3). But since Jesus' Passion and Resurrection, we can say with Paul, "He who did not withhold his own Son, but gave him up for all of us, will he not with him also give us everything else?" (Rom 8:32). We know the answer: God-Love wants to give us everything and does so. And when our contrition asks for and gets God's pardon, sometimes through our brother or sister, praying with our sin becomes giving thanks for such Love. And it creates within us the desire to say a yes as big as the no of our sin. Scripture is precisely the unceasing history of the pardon and the intimacy of God given again and again, from the first to the last verse, and magnified to the extreme in the climax of Jesus' Passion and Resurrection.

For Our Children

We understand that when we help children to pray about their sins, we must not create in them a guilt complex and fear of God (enough events and people in their lives will do that!). But such a prayer is a great opportunity for them to understand contrition, the plea for and the gift of forgiveness. Through that, we must go back again and again to the cornerstone of our faith: Jesus' God is a God of Love and mercy, the God of the Covenant, who *never* repudiates our mutual relationship. Jesus' God is always searching for us, like lost sheep, and always forgives and rejoices when we decide to go back home (Lk 15). And we must always assert that behaviors that hurt love are sins. Thus, prudence is required when we help our children to pray about their sins.

For what concerns contrition and forgiveness, the discovery of freedom and of love given back, the best school is family life (the task of educators is more difficult if the family does not provide such education). Without *ever* putting the children in a situation where they would have to make a public confession, it is always possible to pray as a family or as a group with Scriptures talking about our sins (see Chapter 19, "How Can We Pray, As a Family, As Spouses?"). In a more personalized way, a person other than a family member can help a child to see more clearly the patterns in his/her life that I have described above. The same person can also invite the child to make an effort to gain lucidity and the will to change. I have benefited from such help when I was a teenager, and very often I have seen the value and effectiveness of it each time I have helped children spiritually. Spiritual "assistance" is not reserved to grown-ups only!

In the primary school, we also used some liturgies for

these discoveries, without ever raping the children's hearts. The prayer, something like "God have mercy on us," followed several short stories. These stories described sins of children, with the name of the sin and with a minimum of circumstances. Each story was *always* talking about *something against love.* "John liked very much Paul's crayons. One day, Paul forgot them on a bench, and the boy stole them from him"; "Kathy was jealous of Mary, who looked so beautiful in her skirt. During recess, Kathy mocked Mary spitefully in front of their classmates"; "Tony spilled some paint on the carpet. Nobody saw him. When his mother asked who did it, he lied and said, "It is my little brother"; "In the courtyard, some children beat a younger child. Joseph felt a desire to be mean and did it, too." After each story, we had a silent pause, following a phrase like, "Maybe we have been and behaved like John [Kathy, Tony, Joseph]. If we have, let us express our sorrow to Jesus." And then, the refrain, sung or said by all. We were careful never to use a name that was the name of one of the children of the group, and we always said, before starting the stories, that they were about "our" sins. During the classes about sin, we also show, for instance, that to say bad words is really a sin when they hurt love: "Did you hear the word your dad said when he hit himself with a hammer? What is the difference between saying the same word to somebody?" We did not explain my remarks about our sins being acts to verify our freedom; we thought that experiences in the home were the best way to prepare, at some later date, for this kind of explanation.

The refrain of our liturgy was *always* about asking for forgiveness and being sure of its total gift by God to the contrite heart. We chose some texts, chiefly from the gospels, that prove this ultimate message of Jesus and how much we are loved by God. I have not yet forgotten one little girl, eight years old, who noticed aloud that the Risen Jesus, returned to his disciples, never reminded them of their faults and never said to them, "Repent! Ask for forgiveness!"

Chapter 12

Does Penance Help?

THE RETURN OF FASTING during the sixties and the growing influence of Eastern religions have revived the question of asceticism in prayer life. The most famous spiritual authors have always spoken about penance in connection with prayer. Here is a summary of their teaching. Above all, they assert that an inner penance is more important than an external one: For instance, contrition for our sins is better than fasting. Indeed, some people say that fasting makes our mind more alert, but Isaiah already was very reserved about such a practice (Isa 58). The classic spiritual authors also emphasize that we must be moderate in any physical penance. Their caution has found an echo in the remarks of psychologists about the risks of physical penance, e.g., narcissism, morbid sadomasochism with its subtle autoeroticism or its tendency to punish the body, the reinforcing of a poor self-image or the pride of heroic prowesses, more or less conscious bargaining with God ("I sacrifice this, and you give me that."). The wisdom of ancient and modern specialists invites us to listen to them, while finding a place for penance in our prayer life. For as the experts admit penance can sometimes awaken our fervor, shake off our laziness, and dissolve desolation.

Frugality

In fact, in the previous chapters, I have already answered the question that titles this chapter. If the reader has not noticed it, it is because my point was made subtly. The penance I implied was a kind of *frugality,* which means that we use everything with a careful management that never goes overboard. Or as Shakespeare put it, we must "acquire and beget a temperance that may give [life] smoothness." Let me elaborate.

When I mentioned "selecting" and "staying with" a text, it was a call to avoid praying with everything and to wait patiently for a revelation. My exhortation to be comfortable with the body excluded slouching. My advice about the length of time for prayer precluded greed or laxness. In the method of meditation, the intellect is invited "to fast" when the heart wants to talk; in contemplation, it is the text that tells us which character we are, and we "fast" from any desire to be the one we like more; and if we are sent back to our past wounds, it is far from any delight; to pray with a mantra does not fuel our search for intellectual or emotional pleasure. To accept silence is really to fast from all the "noises" we like to create in prayer. So frugality is a form of penance, an inner and humble one. And let me expand on that idea, using our five physical senses as illustration.

Our prayer is difficult if we look at too many pictures, paintings, statues, icons, flowers (in a museum, after a while, we are saturated). We blunt our capacity to hear if we use too much music, too many songs. And when it comes to smell, I have just to remember the day I was in a group that had to leave a chapel because we had burned too much incense! Our sense of touch? Pray in a very, very comfortable chair, and you are going to fall into a deep sleep. We touch the ground when we walk, but walking too much or too fast removes pleasure; it is so, too, if we try to pray while walking. Blessed be God, we cannot keep too many things or something too heavy in our hands. As for the mouth, let me just remind you that after a meal with too much food or drink, we need to nap. As for words, I'll quote Jesus: "In your prayer, do not rattle on like the pagans" (Mt 6:7. A mantra is not rattling on, for we repeat the same one.). When we consume too much with our five physical senses, our spiritual senses cannot function easily.

So, frugality consists in avoiding "too much," even when excess seems motivated by the best intentions (after all, the road to hell is proverbially paved with such intentions). For example, a priest who was in a directed retreat with me asked for permission to fast; I agreed. The following day, he told me his surprise because his prayer periods had not been fruitful. We looked for the cause, and he said that he had not eaten or drunk anything for twenty-four hours! He had exhausted his body. He corrected his behavior, and his prayer improved enormously. In my book *Is God Deaf?* I show that we need a minimum of signs, and that means that we never use a maximum. Concerning penance in prayer, I prefer to repeat what I said earlier, "Better to be complacent but to hear than to be ascetical and deaf." In fact, we must find a balance between not enough and too much. My friend the priest did not eat and drink enough; others would eat and drink too much. The middle way, called *temperance* by our predecessors, *moderation* by the ancients, protects us from addictions that can exist even in spiritual life. It is said that Ignatius of Loyola, a master about prayer, asserted, "It is dangerous to pray too much." The balance between formal prayer life and ordinary daily activities in the monks' lifestyle demonstrates the same wisdom.

I abandon the vainglory of spectacular exploits to spiritual macho-athletes. As I explained in Chapter 4, "While I Pray, What Do I Do With My Body?," I left this heroism when, at the age of eighteen, I made my first seven-day directed retreat. For the first three days, I prayed on my knees, and they hurt. When the retreat master told me to stop this penance, he confirmed the message my body had tried to make me understand: "Enough is enough!"

Nevertheless, I urge you to heed the advice of the best spiritual writers about our times of laziness or desolation. But I would merely say, "When we see that our fervor is gone, that we have become lazy or that desolation is there, let us go back to our usual fidelity in prayer." It is ordinarily a sufficient penance to start again a regular prayer life, to stay as long as we have decided, and to wait patiently, because it is not always easy to do so. Very often, to return to the most material faithfulness puts everything back into place. Of course, because all deeds of our life influence our prayer, it is wise to check out what is wrong in our daily actions when prayer seems to be unproductive; and, if we change our behaviors, we face penance!

Simplicity

Through time, frugality filters our prayer. It slows down our activity, prunes and purifies its content of what is superfluous, removes what may still clutter our vision, and leaves us with a few thoughts or images, sounds or words. One day we discover that we are satisfied with less food and fewer drinks, and our prayer is essentially *simplicity*. On the news last night, I saw Nelson Mandela celebrating, in front of his supporters, the end of apartheid and the birth of a new South Africa. He danced. It was a slow and peaceful dance, with a graceful and serene pace, even though his heart was undoubtedly exulting. Nothing in that dance resembled the frenzied screams, hugs, and applause of contestants winning $11,249 on some TV shows. Of course, Nelson Mandela is in his seventies. But also, his joy was rooted in twenty years of prison, in decades of battle and the suffering he had shared with so many in South Africa. This dance may be our prayer someday.

For it also becomes simpler and simpler, fashioned by years of sorrows and joys, battles and truces, etc. It is far from any gymnastics or aerobic sessions, from the kaleido-

scope of fireworks, from any grand opera. We are closer to
the sober liturgy of a Trappist convent than to the luxurious
one of Benedictine monks, to the plain Roman style than to
the gimcrackery of rococo excess. Our eyes are satisfied with
the same icon, a simple picture (like the art of Picasso and
Matisse in their last drawings — lines only). One single song
or piece of music feeds us, and that is all. Very few words are
in our heart. We are no longer running back and forth in our
prayer. Rather, we are walking peacefully and silently along
a deep river, hand in hand, with a very old friend, the only
One who has known us since we were born.

We are with God like two old lovers who say a lot to one
another in three words, a smile, a touch on the hand, for we
know each other. Together, we have passed through joys and
sorrows, laughter and tears, and we have understood that
henceforth we are forever one. The Martha, "anxious and
upset about many things," we have been joins the Mary we
all are deep down inside of ourselves, and we seat ourselves
at Jesus' feet peacefully and silently. We have learned that
"one thing only is necessary"; we have found it, and we enjoy
it. And God does it, too (Lk 10:38–42).

For Our Children

It is worse than useless to put any physical penance in
children's prayer, for this can effectively turn them away
from praying for life (and what picture of God would they
get?). But I think it necessary to educate children in frugality, exactly as intelligent parents train the mouths and the
appetites of their little ones. Concerning prayer itself, frugality will help children to be attentive, for everybody knows
that youngsters can be easily distracted by anything. I have
already sown the seeds of frugality for our children in previous chapters. I emphasized the importance of continually
repeating the love God has for us, and keeping ourselves unceasingly and frugally prayer-centered. I spoke about pauses
of silence in all prayer times; I stressed the desirability of not

losing children in too many details; I said that it was good to sing the same refrain and to read a text with a neutral tone of voice out of respect for the child; it was with a few short stories and not a lot that we prayed about our sins in the primary school; all of this is frugality. A very important simplification with the youngest children is to talk primarily about Jesus (a God who is One and Three is already complicated for us, so let us simplify; and also we want to educate them as Christians, not just as theists).

Some adults prepare liturgies for children that are too complicated, to the point that I wonder who wants to be satisfied. To do so follows too much the modern tendency toward an information overload that overwhelms us with noises, commercials, etc. We don't serve children's best interests when we do the same. We go against the spontaneity of a child's heart that prays to God in simplicity, and we don't prepare the heart of the adult to come.

Around Christmastime, some years ago, I was visiting from church to church with some children, in Marseilles, France. In Provence, it was the custom to make the rounds of the different crèches, i.e., Nativity scenes. In one church, we saw not only the Infant, Mary and Joseph, the donkey and the cow, several shepherds and a lot of sheep, the three kings and their camels loaded with presents, and their followers, but also all the additional characters that are traditional to Provence — the *"santons"*: the ravished one, the Gypsy, the miller and his wife, the blind man and his son, the knife grinder, the fishermen, the woman selling fish, etc. You can imagine the reactions of the children to all this human pageantry. Oh, it was gorgeous, but it was impossible to pray formally there! In another church, we found, Mary, Joseph, and, between them, Jesus. Silence came by itself and praying was easy, for the Essential was there: He, in our human flesh.

Chapter 13

What Can I Do When I Am Distracted in Prayer?

ONE DISTURBING PROBLEM in our prayer life is that we have distractions. Many times we don't know what to do with that plague! But some distractions have value, if we learn what to do with them. Usually, we experience two kinds of distractions: Some are just "silly," and some have serious underpinnings.

"Silly" Distractions

I am praying in front of the ocean. It's helping me to get a sense of God's infinity. Suddenly, I see myself water-skiing! Or I am praying with David, fighting Goliath, in 1 Samuel 17; all of a sudden, I am a boxing champion in a ring. In order to get rid of the distraction, I have simply to return to the text or the mental picture I was praying with before the distraction jumped into my mind. For those of us whose imagination is fairly inventive, it will be like returning our attention again and again to a friend who's speaking to us while the TV is still on and showing an interesting program. If the distraction persists, we can try to become like two people: the director of the movie and the spectator at the movie. As the spectator, we say to the director, "You want to show a movie? Fine, go ahead. As for me, I'm not interested!" Very often the movie disappears, for we don't consent to it.

If our imagination is great, we give it something to chew on connected with our prayer; while beginning our prayer period, we give ourselves a mental image fitting the subject of our prayer, like Jesus on the cross if we pray about the Passion or the disciples around him if we pray about the Last Supper. It might be a real picture, like an icon we put before us, so our imagination stays quiet. If this does not work, we must learn to be like a child on his father's lap while the father is visiting a moment with friends (Ps 131). The talking in the background does not prevent the child from simply being there and listening to the heart beating for him in Dad's breast.

The worst is when we never have any distractions. It means very probably that we are working too hard to stay focused. Therefore, we don't pray in a relaxed way that permits our being to breathe freely. We want to force the issue, from fear of letting go within ourselves, from fear of allowing God to speak freely to us. Usually, such a tension makes prayer life tiring. I once asked a retreatant for whom nothing was happening in his prayer times, "What kind of distractions do you experience?" He said, "None." When he explained how he was praying, we realized that his energy was so consumed by avoiding distractions that he could not "hear" anything else. Later on, he discovered that he did not want to hear what God had to say. So, somehow, to have distractions is a sign of a healthy spiritual behavior in prayer.

Serious Distractions

This kind of distraction concerns something objectively important in our life. One person came on retreat with me three weeks after losing her child. This loss was unceasingly present in her prayer periods.

I invited her to try to put that aside, as calmly and gently as possible, and to say to God, "If you want, we can talk about that later. For I am not sure that this question that preoccupies me is really uppermost for you when you look at me." This is a way to try to remain free, since maybe we don't see the forest for the trees. If we are too close to a tree, it covers our whole horizon and seems like the essential thing; if we step backward, we see the whole forest, and the tree falls into place with the rest. And it is also a way to let God be free.

But suppose the distraction still remains, in spite of our attempts to remain free. It is like an *obsession* that cannot be chased away. Then, we must pray *with it,* making it the very object of our prayer. We go to God with it; we ruminate over it in front of God. We are, somehow, saying to God, "Here I am with my problem. Tell me why it is such an obsession." It is helpful sometimes to bring it to God in a setting given by the Scriptures and fitting it. It is a death: I pray with Lazarus' death, for instance (Jn 11). I have been betrayed: I pray with Peter's denial or Judas' betrayal. My life is a painful ordeal: I take Isaiah 43:1–5.

With *time,* the distraction usually slowly settles in the sight of God and takes on its true dimensions. Already the distraction is no longer preoccupying us; rather *we* occupy ourselves with it. The control of the situation is now in our hands. Progressively, we obtain information about why this specific event is so important for us. The mother I mentioned discovered that the death of her child had made her one of the many mothers who had known the same ordeal — women she had never thought of as long as she had not been personally hit. Then she realized that she hurt because she was grieving the loss of her "property," her baby doll, more than grieving a young life cut off too soon. Her obsession was tenacious because something deep within her had been touched: indifference and possessiveness. But what I have just said sends us back to the "silly" distractions.

Obsessions

I remember myself reading the written notes of a retreatant after her verbal report. She had put down several times "silly song." "What does that mean?" I asked. "Oh, I forgot to tell you. All day long I was haunted by a silly song." "Which song?" I replied. She gave me the words of the song. They *were* silly, like words for a child. "Where does that song come from?" I asked. She said, "It is a song my dad used to sing to me as a lullaby every night." She went back to the song and prayed about it, and she understood that she had to grieve the death of her father, who had died ten years earlier.

I can now generalize our discovery. First, in front of any distraction, let us try to become free and to let God be free, for, as I have explained above, God might have something else to say. Then, if the distraction persists, we pray about it, because God has some information to reveal to us *through* what is seemingly disturbing our prayer. It is in fact, already, the prayer of our deepest being. And God knows that.

For Our Children

It is wise to accept that young children are easily distracted! It is our task to make prayer with them simple, short, and interesting, to avoid distractions. However, in a conversation with them, like the one described in Chapter 3, "Why Doesn't Scripture Talk to Me?," it would be very good to talk *about* distractions, in order to say without judgment that they are a fact of prayer life. After all, every child experiences distractions in the classroom (and all of us in other instances), and we have enough people making that a source of guilt for them. I don't think that it is appropriate to do the same when it concerns our relationship with God. I remember the sigh of relief of a group of children when one adult said, "Oh, I was distracted by that dog that did not stop barking outside!" It is also beneficial not to put a ban on children's imagination, the root of their creativity; but let us teach them to learn progressively to own it, to manage it as a part of themselves. This will eventually be fruitful for schoolwork and for life. Was Mozart distracted when he prayed because he was composing symphonies?

With older children, talking about distractions can help them to become aware of what dwells within themselves and profit from it. In the primary school, because one of the children had been distracted during our liturgy by the death of her turtle, we were able to share all together about death and its impact on our life (the children reacted very well, for many had lost a hamster, a bird, and also a grandpa or their mother). I also recall the fruitfulness of a conversation with a prayer group of teenagers where mutual trust had been built, about their distractions concerning their sweethearts: We ended up talking about the beauty of reciprocal attraction for human beings, as the channel for friendship and love, as one of the most precious ways to understand God's covenant with us.

With older teenagers, what I have said about distractions can be used as it is described.

Chapter 14

How Can I Pray When I Am Too Busy?

T HIS IS A FREQUENT QUESTION. This chapter assumes it is being asked with honesty. For sometimes it is masking a more or less conscious refusal or fear of encountering God methodically and regularly, or it may simply be an excuse for our laziness. And very often the problem is only proof that God does not interest us. But I want to offer here a solution for people who are objectively busy and yet sincerely desire to pray, like many I have worked with over the years, ordained ministers, the consecrated, or laypersons.

The daily schedule of monks is structured in such a way that their prayer times are protected. All other believers are not so lucky. However, the motto of Saint Benedict and the monks, *"Ora et Labora"* ("Pray *and* work"), gives us somehow the two principles that must rule our prayer life. We must give priority to our personal meetings with God, *"Ora,"* but we must take into account the other necessities of our life — our work, for instance (*"Labora"*). How can we do *both*, signified by the *"et,"* all of us who don't live in an abbey, without knowing scrupulosity or complacency? "I should pray more," or, "After all, my work is a form of prayer," summarize such extremes. This book is about the means of prayer; I won't elaborate on the question, as I did in *Is God Deaf?* where I answer the

same question through Paul's advice, "Pray without ceasing"
(1 Thess 5:17).

A Pattern

Two friends of mine revealed to me the pattern I am going to
explain. It is a Love story, as prayer is. Let us call them Pierre
and Mary.

Pierre and Mary had four children, between two and
twelve years of age, when I met them. They were very active with and for their sons and daughters, taking part in
parents' committees at school, for instance; they were also
members of a Christian spiritual organization I was chaplain
of, with a monthly meeting. Mary, a housewife, supervised
all the volunteers supplying recreation to hospitalized children in the city (population: around 1 million). Pierre was a
civil engineer, head of a department in a firm of public works.
He belonged also to the Jaycees of the city and founded an
organization of French families welcoming foreign managers
present for a while in the region. And they were present to a
network of friends and relatives, as anybody is. Rather busy,
both of them!

I was struck by their way of expressing their love to each
other. I knew that love was their first priority. But I progressively admired more and more how they managed it without
forgetting family, acquaintances, work, etc.

Any opportunity was for them a possibility to give a quick
kiss, to say a word of love, to exchange a furtive caress. The
few minutes offered to them at breakfast, or at lunch, always included something showing their mutual attachment.
"You look tired, are you?" "Love you, running!" "What
was your day like? Tell me quick because I have to go." A
twinkle of an eye, a special hug, a smile of complicity, a pressure on the hand, two feet brushing each other, expressed
their tenderness for each other, even in public. They never
stopped giving each other love, but they did it according to

what their schedule, the place, the circumstances, allowed them to do. One minute here, ten there, thirty another time, a very quick shot, but *always* a proof of love. Sometimes it was just some crumbs, other times it was several slices, but love was their daily bread. And once in a while, it was a cake!

Because *one evening a week,* always the same one, was sacred for them. Only a very urgent necessity would make them renounce that special time. They told me that the menu of those hours was not always the same, but that it was always made of freedom and enjoyment, relaxation and intimacy. To eat in a restaurant, to play a tennis game, to go and see a movie or a play, to attend a concert, to take a long walk along the river, were the dishes they used to concoct together. Or sometimes it was just a long evening spent quietly at home. All of that prepared and started the first hours of the night when their love was sometimes giving its most delicious fruit. In their own words, it was a long *liturgy* of intimacy savored step by step. And they tried to keep the same structure during the year, although less systematically. They attempted to take a day a month for themselves, and one week of vacation a year without their children. Concerning these last points, I was struck that they had discovered by themselves an old custom of religious life: the monthly recollection day and the annual retreat.

For years, I saw them living that pattern. It worked very well. So they inspired me, and I applied their invention to prayer life for busy people. And all the feedback I have heard says that it is very effective.

Always Praying

If a love is not expressed, it becomes enfeebled; if it is not shown externally, it grows doubtful for the beloved, but also for the lover. So it is with prayer and our relationship with God. Therefore, we must always pray formally and regularly in order to prove our love to God, and to prove to our-selves that God really counts. If we don't, what does that mean? For instance, if we remain with a spontaneous kind of prayer only, are we reluctant to generously give time and our conscious attention to God?

Therefore, we must give priority to prayer in our life. This says clearly, "God, Love, first served." We can translate this priority like this: *Never* accept a day without a minimum of conscious relation with God, without a minimum of formal prayer. However, we must act with the available time we have. Monday, it will be ten minutes; Tuesday, twenty are possible; Wednesday, five only; Thursday looks so loaded with unavoidable tasks that we'll be able only to say the Our Father just before falling asleep, etc. This example shows that we don't spend a day without meeting God, but we're realistic. This time might seem like nothing to some people, but it gives us a significant piece of information. It means that God is very important to us, because it proves that we *never* forget God.

A Time for a "Liturgy"

I said, "God is very important to us." This must be visibly proven sometimes, because, even if we implement the above suggestion, it is still too often only implied in our daily life. So, let us put aside, once a week, a good length of time for savoring, as Pierre and Mary did, a long liturgy with and for God. Around two hours, for instance. But it must be a time long enough so that we can give our being the leisure to un-fold more systematically and peacefully its capacity to love God. A time that allows us to wait and to hear God without being disturbed by anything. Because it is a long while, we can read Scriptures (for instance, the Passion during Lent) or a nourishing spiritual book; we can listen to some music or songs helpful for our prayer; and we can enjoy finally a long moment of formal prayer (if we already pray one hour a day, and I have known many busy people praying that much, this pattern is not necessary).

And, still following Pierre and Mary's pattern, we do the same for the year. Once in a while, we take one full day for God. Once a year, it is a "vacation" with God, at home or in a summer house, in a retreat house or in a monastery. Friends of mine used to make a retreat in their trailer on the beach or in a chalet in the Alps, even under a tent, during their vacation; spouses or friends, they enjoyed together long moments of solitude and silence with God.

Such hours or days, when everything is done for encountering God, signify *priority time*. A priority given to mutual presence with Love. We must, from time to time, give time to this priority time. A moment where the other, God here, becomes the center of our attention, care and concern, as Pierre was for Mary, and Mary for Pierre, in the pattern they revealed to me. A time that is no longer spent with many things or people, but all for God, the Unique One who is eventually necessary (Lk 10:42). And we get the information that we want and we are able to take time to love and to be loved.

The Fruit

This management of time delivers us from any guilt complex, because we can always say to ourselves, "I have given priority to my relationship with God, and so to God." We have seriously followed the monks' message, "God first." But also we can recognize, "I did what was possible for me at that time," without struggling with, "I should have ironed, finished this project, done my homework, written that letter, etc." Thus, we'll be sure that we have not let ourselves be ruled by fear, refusal of God, laziness, or other undesirable emotions.

And, furthermore, I believe that God, who knows all of that, will give us the same graces expected by monks in their

scheduled prayer life, through the limited but organized time
we have. God, who treats a monk as someone who lives in
an abbey, can treat us as busy people living in the frame and
the work according to the schedules of a lay world.

After all, when we love a man or a woman, we always find
time, short or long, to meet and be with him or her.

For Our Children

Children have to learn that praying is not just for Sundays in
church and for a few minutes before going to bed. It is necessary to let them know that they can talk with God at any time
and as long as they want (easy for a generation that loves to
spend time on the phone with friends!). "When you want,
you can always say to Jesus what is in your mind or heart,
and give him a call," said a friend of mine to her daughter,
who understood perfectly the message. I remember my conversations, at fourteen, with Jesus all the way to school. It
is "to walk humbly with God" as Micah speaks about; it
is the disciples talking with the Risen One on their way to
Emmaus, once again realized for our children (Mic 6:8; Lk
24:13–35). This kind of companionship teaches children that
God is always with us and always interested in everything
about our life. This way of praying will be helped by morning and evening prayer, by saying grace, by going to church
once a week, moments that can be the equivalents of the "liturgy" I explained (see also Chapter 19, "How Can We Pray
As a Family, As Spouses?").

We also have another means of showing our children this
lifestyle of prayer. It is for us adults to dare to share the kind
of prayer that suddenly rises within us before any event (and
that allows us to ask our children if one prayer, and which
one, has come to them at the same moment). The challenge
is not to exaggerate, or to put God or Jesus into anything,
at any time; that can depreciate the invocation. Some people
have a tendency to invoke God so often and so easily that we
wonder about the depth of their spontaneity; but some others

mention God so rarely before their children that we question how much God might be a part of their life. Too much is too much, but not enough is not enough, for ourselves and chiefly for our children. We face here a question of honesty, wisdom, and balance.

Chapter 15

How Can I Pray,
I Am So Sick?

I WILL CONSIDER three stages in regard to illness: before, during, and after. *Before* means before a feared diagnosis, a serious treatment, or surgery. *During* evokes clearly the days under the power of the disease. *After* refers to convalescence. But I'll start by saying that when the question, which I have often heard, concerns a physical sickness, it always surprises me, because, for me, the answer has been obvious for a long time and always starts like this: "Don't worry, *your body already prays.*" This simple assertion will explain many things I am going to say. At the end of the chapter, I'll consider the question when it is asked because of an emotional ordeal.

An Immense Tenderness

The content of Chapter 4, "While I Pray, What Do I Do With My Body?," finds its ultimate meaning here. I spoke about praying in a comfortable bodily posture. Here are the consequences of this principle for before, during, and after a disease.

If we believe that we are our body, our being *is,* in sickness, *this* suffering body. So, the best advice is: In order to allow our "suffering-me-body" to exhale, to "pray," we must give it all the comfort we can. "Take care of yourself as much as you can first of all," I say to the patient, "means take care of your body." I spoke above about praying freely with our body. Here, I translate these words, "to let our body express itself, to 'pray' freely." It is first of all not to overtax our body by trying to pray the way we do when we are well. For our body gives us information to take into account: "I hurt!" A peculiar God speaks clearly through our body. It is "the God of the lowly, the helper of the oppressed, the supporter of the weak, the protector of the forsaken, the savior of those without hope," the God who wants to rescue "the poor who [cry] out for help," "those in extremity," the father of the needy," the God who "hears the cry of the poor" (Jdt 9:11; Job 29:12–16; Ps 34:7). This God begs us to be our own Good Samaritan, and nothing else (Lk 10:25–37). Jesus asserts that the second commandment is like the first, and he quotes Leviticus: "You shall love your neighbor *as yourself*" (Mt 22:37–39; Lev 19:18). Often, it is difficult for us to understand that "love God" = "love your neighbor" = "love yourself." If there is a time in our life when this truth must be easy and necessary to accept, if not to live, it is certainly when an illness attacks us. We *must* then love with an immense tenderness our nearest neighbor, our body. Thus, we are for ourselves the first sacrament of the compassion that is God. What other behavior could God love most at that time? Compassion will remove a temptation for us who are with the patient. Sometimes we think that he/she is too much like a crying baby. But not only are we outside of that body that suffers in ways other bodies cannot share, but we are there not for judgment but for compassion.

Thus, we have to do what is possible for relaxing our body (helped by people around us), in order to free the word that rises from it toward God. If we can, with simplicity, let us free that word with others, too, for it is a source of precious information about where we are emotionally and spiritually. I remember visiting an old priest who was sick: He usually talked about his sufferings, in a few words without a big show, and then asked me about my ministry. So if our body complains, we give it time for complaining; our body is restless, we welcome it agitated; our body is feverish, we make its fever our own; our body is exhausted, we abandon it to the care of who is nursing us, etc. And if we can, like the old priest, we try to be present to people. But medical care being assured, we don't try to be other than our suffering body right now. It is already enough to suffer, and so it is not useful to add the pain of any inner division within ourselves. I repeat again what I said in Chapter 4, "Better to be complacent but to hear, than to be ascetical and deaf!" But to hear in this sense means to hear our body, and God speaking through it. Why would we use with God a language other than our body's? Can we have for ourselves the tenderness we give our cherished ones when they are suffering? And let us eschew the vanity of playing the stoic or Superman or Superwoman (however, I have also known patients who kept their laments for me, in order to spare their loved ones; I applauded such a proof of love, but it is important not to isolate ourselves in mute suffering).

This prayer may take confounding forms for someone who has never suffered. One morning, I heard my neighbor raging behind the wall; I won't tell you what mantra was coming out of his mouth! I went to see him. He was twisting with pain on his bed because of nephritic colic produced by kidney stones. Days later, we laughed about his unorthodox litany. An intelligent priest, he was free with God in his "prayer," the prayer of his body. I think also of a Carmelite sister who, during her deadly disease, dared to complain. She was an inspiration for the whole floor of the hospital, for she had accepted to be just a sorrowful human being. She did not pretend to be a saintly martyr! A friend of mine was swearing a lot because of his suffering, saying the French curse, "Name of God!" ("*Nom de Dieu!*"), for he was from France. After a while, he realized how biblical the expression was; it then became a prayer imploring God's name. Are we scandalized by these "prayers"? In fact, many things would be simpler if we would better love ourselves and our body, and therefore its peculiar prayer in sickness. Maybe illness would be more bearable. For instance, the immense tenderness I spoke about can push aside any anger against our own body when it is ill. After all, this body would not mind not knowing what is happening to itself!

Concerning the time before a diagnosis or surgery, it is good to give our body, if we can, the grace of not adding to its sufferings the nightmares of our imagination. The whole of ourselves will also benefit from this clemency. "I'll be told that I have cancer, AIDS, tuberculosis, etc." Magic words, loaded with apprehensions, which will just increase the torture of our body and ourselves. If some people deny terrible possibilities or are not conscious of them, many of us are prone to cultivating imaginary fears (meaning products of our imagination), even though some commercials insist, "My doctor said it was not a stomach ulcer but just heartburn or indigestion!" Better then to pray with facts and time: "God, as long as I don't know for sure, I'll try not to picture the worst possibility, and to take one day at a time." If this is not sufficient, Scriptures like Isaiah 43:1–5, for instance, make us look at the future with faith: *If* we pass through raging waters and fire, God will be with us (our memories of past experiences of God's fidelity can reinforce our hope). Some psalms also contain verses that fit this time of anxiety: 13, 22, 23, 25, and others.

During our convalescence, it is still good to keep the same tenderness for our body. But we can also enter with it into the multiple grace of that time. The grace of seeing our worst fears going away, the grace of feeling more and more alive, the grace of slowly welcoming our body and our mind back to us and others again, the grace of an unavoidable passivity, full now of serenity and trust in the dawn of spring. And sometimes the grace of emerging from hell and being back "home." The grace of a thousand "Thank yous." Because things are getting better, we often forget to hear God

saying all of that within ourselves, within our body. The
Spirit of Jesus' Father is rejoicing within us for our cure, as
it happened in all the witnesses of Jesus' miracles. The list
of Scriptures that can be our prayer during our convalescence is too long to mention, but all can be summarized by,
"O Lord, my God, I cried to you for help, and you have
healed me. O Lord, you brought up my soul from Sheol, re-
stored me to life from among those gone down to the Pit"
(Ps 30:2–3).

If Formal Prayer Is Possible

When we have given comfort and freedom of speech to our
body, the question of formal prayer might arise. We have to
take it seriously, but with the adjustments and precautions
required by the time of sickness. Quickly, I review what I said
in chapters 4 and 6.

Methods

Of course, everything depends on the individual circumstances: the gravity of the disease, the intensity of the pain,
the place where the patient is, etc. It is difficult to pray
with our intellect when we are ill. So, we do what we can
with the method of meditation. We can slowly read passages
of Scripture that have usually consoled us. The Passion of
Jesus is often the best text when illness and sufferings are
great. Of course, we always give priority to the *colloquy*, the
expression of our heart.

Contemplation might be easier if our imagination is not
locked by the suffering as our intellect is. But often we can
become one of the characters of the story without too much
trouble: I think of someone who easily saw himself as the
wounded man in the ditch of the parable of the Good Samaritan, or of a woman who was Mary looking at her crucified
son — she was both of them (Lk 10:25–37; Jn 19:25). Here,

we use our five senses. We can merely look at a picture, an icon that is inspiring and calming; adjusting the light helps. We can listen to some music or songs that soften our mind and comfort our heart, or to someone reading appeasing texts to us, or we can remain in silence if any noise hurts us. Flowers that smell and look good (they remind us of people loving us), a bit of perfume around or on us, are not things to disregard. Touching is important at that time. Patients need to be "touched" in every sense of the word, with gentle, silent, tender repeated caresses. We can also touch, without a word, a rosary, a little religious statue, a crucifix, a baby bear, etc. I have seen patients kissing objects they held in their hands, reciting psalms they knew by heart, humming softly the same song or mantra (here we have the last method I described, to pray with a melody).

Finally, if we believe in it, receiving the Body and Blood of Christ might be a very special opportunity for praying. With him so close to our suffering body and our disturbed heart, a silent dialogue can take place within ourselves that cannot be described. Literally, it is at the deepest level of ourselves that God is then working. Indeed, many patients have testified how much such a "presence" has been helpful for them.

Here is one of the best proofs for me of the value of prayer in the time of sickness. A woman was making with me the Spiritual Exercises of Ignatius of Loyola in a thirty-day retreat. After three weeks, she had to be hospitalized. Many were surprised that I visited her every day because she remained in retreat; and they were even more surprised that it was fruitful. But I must explain that her hospitalization took place just when, in the process of the Spiritual Exercises, we had reached the time to pray with Jesus' Passion.

As we see, solutions to the problem of praying when we are sick are many. We have just to know them, to have practiced them, and to find the ones that fit us the best when we are ill. People who are around us can also help us with their suggestions and creativity. Forty years ago, I learned my first lessons in this matter during fourteen days and nights at the bedside of my mother while she was dying.

Feelings

It is good to pray formally, if it is possible, because illness sometimes releases within us feelings difficult to manage. For example, we may feel guilt for our excesses if they caused the disease (e.g., cirrhosis of the liver due to alcoholism), for the worries we have created for our family, for being an impossible patient; resentment against our body that escapes our control and hurts us, against doctors and nurses, against God (for this last point, see my book, *May I Hate God?*). We really need to be helped by God. When we pray, we see God accepting our contrition, forgiving us, and giving us peace, making us accept our powerlessness or bad temper, and embracing our rage with understanding and compassion. Indeed, it is a blessing if someone is there like the angel in Jesus' agony, is there as a flesh-and-blood sacrament of Jesus' God (Lk 22:43). Often also, God reveals what lies behind our feelings and gives us information for conversions. We were winners: It is time to accept that life is not always a success; we liked to control: The time has come to discover that we, too, depend on others; we were so full of lust for immediate and superficial satisfactions that we ignored the warnings of our body: Now we are ready to change; we used to put our trust in money, power, fame, or others idols: Today we have to accept some form of poverty. Sickness has been a time of conversion for many people, for it is a strong spiritual experience. It becomes even more so when it is brought to God in prayer.

    That is why the question of this chapter must be answered in the best possible way for the patient, whether ourselves or another whom we help. Speaking about feelings leads to the same question, but this time when we are dealing with an emotional sickness.

God Knows...

When we are emotionally very disturbed, *if we still think of praying formally, let us do what we can.* I say "if" and "what we can" because we must deal with ourselves with tenderness and compassion. The content of this chapter remains valid and can be tried by the emotionally ill. Praying with the psalms may be especially helpful in this situation, for they cover almost all the feelings we might experience, but all directed toward God. Therefore we can pray in any emotional state with them (an appendix in my book *May I Hate God?* gives other quotations of Scriptures). However, distress can distort our perception, and we must anticipate that it may be impossible to perceive what is going on in our relationship with God. I experienced this with friends and relatives when they were passing through emotional ordeals.

- Angela was falling into a deep depression. One night, "before God" (I never knew what she meant), she said to herself, "O.K., accept it. You are having a nervous breakdown." Strangely, the following day, she started recovering. I said to myself, "To admit reality is a way of praying."

- I whispered again and again the same short prayer in the ear of my mother, while keeping her hand in mine. Once in a while, it seemed that her lips were moving and her fingers were pressuring mine. Can we see this as prayer? A mutual prayer?

- Steven had been severely suicidal several times. He used to read very slowly Jesus' Passion, and thus was able to recover from each attack.

- Robert was in the fetal posture and mute in bed. His son was playing some religious songs on the tape player.

Robert had begged, "When I am in very bad shape, please, play this cassette."

- In rage, Sarah spoke about her youth. Repeatedly raped by her father, from the ages of seven to eighteen, she eventually became pregnant, and was rejected by the residents of her small town. She threw at me, "What do you say?" I replied, "I, what can I say? Tell him, he only can answer you," while pointing my finger to a crucifix on the wall. Later, she told me that face-to-face with Jesus crucified, she was answered.

- After thirty seconds, as usual, Katherine started sobbing. But she had warned me in our first encounter, "Don't worry. I am neurotic, and I always do that." I discovered in her a person spiritually free despite her disturbed psyche. And I knew this freedom was given her through prayer (Which kind? That was her mystery and her God's).

- Scott was not talking at all, but twisting unceasingly a crucifix between his fingers.

And so many others.

So, when we are emotionally sick, we do what we can — we, the patient, and also we the loving ones or caretakers of the patient who are there. Above all, let us *believe* that if the word of a suffering body is heard by God, no less is the expression of a tormented psyche, be the word formal or not. And we must believe that God answers it. That is what happened when God listened to Jesus' anguish in the Garden of Olives and to his pierced body on Golgotha.

For Our Children

In sickness, little children are just suffering bodies. So they "pray," in their own way and by their own mystery. My faith says, "God hears the child's cry" (Gen 21:17). We have to do the same, to hear and to grant their "prayer" for security and relief. We must therefore be all arms, all tenderness, all caresses, all kisses, and all reassuring words only, as God's merciful hands and voice. And we suffer and pray for and with them.

When they are older, we do the same, but we can also try to help them to pray more formally with all the means I have described, but adjusted to their age. Giving them the opportunity to receive Communion, if it is our faith and if it fits the child, is a splendid help for their prayer. But also, we use stories, songs, objects they can hold in their hands, mantras, prayers they know by heart. Any form of verbal prayer is somehow easy, if we don't pray too much or too long.

As a teenager, I was once a part of a group that went to visit a young friend who was sick, and to perform before him some scenes of a religious play we had prepared for a parish celebration. I am sure that it was a prayer. We may also invite children who are ill to do by themselves what we have done with them. The most essential thing is to communicate our immense care and tenderness, but it is good to attempt formal prayer if we know that it is going to help our children. However, we must be ready for surprises, whether funny or tragic.

- Albert's whole body was itching. Being at the end of her resources, his mother said to him, "Pray to Jesus that it will go away." And we heard a thousand times, "Jesus, make it so that it no longer itches." And all of a sudden, "O Jesus, scratch me!"

- Oliver, five years of age, was slowly dying from leukemia. One day his mother said to him, while showing him a picture of Jesus crucified, "See, the thorns on his head are like the shots you get." "Yes, Mom, but for him it did not last so long."

- At four, Paula was dying from a cancerous brain tumor. In addition to everything we could do, a little music box was playing unceasingly a melody she had always liked (now, the music box is on my desk).

• My first spiritual helper, a priest of my parish, told me how staggering it had been for him to see a ten-year-old boy die in his arms and scream, "I don't want to die!"

Chapter 16

May I Ask God for Everything?

T HE ABOVE QUESTION and the question of the next chapter are one for me.* It is obvious that the answer to "Will God Grant My Prayer?" depends on what we reply to the question "May I Ask God For Everything?" It is easy to prove the connection between the questions, if we go to the extreme: If we have no right to ask for anything, we have no reason to question if our prayer has not been granted; on the other hand, if we have the right to plead, we can ask questions if we think that our wishes have not been granted.

We must admit that asking for something makes us feel uneasy. Some people refuse to treat God like Santa Claus. A noble sentiment, but Jesus himself says, "Until now you have not asked for anything in my name. Ask and you will receive, so that your joy may be complete" (Jn 16:24). He had already said, "So I tell you, whatever you ask for in prayer, believe that you have received it, and it will be yours" (Mk 11:24). In the gospel, he himself petitions. Indeed, the Lord's Prayer, which he gave us, is full of supplications. And let us keep in mind that when Jesus was asked, "Teach us to pray," he did not reply, "Give thanks," or "Praise God" (Lk 11:1). On the contrary, he taught his followers to petition. So, can we ask God for something? My answer is, "Of course!"

---

*That is why the remarks *For Our Children* will be found at the end of the following chapter.

113

Since the Beginning

It is impossible for us not to beg, for petition was our first "prayer." Asking has been rooted in us since we were born, and that explains why it has never ceased. We ask for Mom's breast, a milk bottle, food, candies, toys, raises, medical care, justice, promotions, respect, tenderness, understanding, and so forth. This form of prayer is unavoidable because we are needy beings. We would all worry about a child who never begged for anything. So let us respect prayer of petition that reveals to us that we are always unsatisfied, never finished. Those who are full will never be hungry for anything or anybody. Why would they reach out to others or to God?

When we pray for something, do we picture our prayer from God's perspective? As a guideline, let us look at a child's plea from the parents' side. Our own parents sometimes made us reflect about our request, or postponed its satisfaction, or said no. If they hadn't refused us, we would have become insatiable tyrants, with no strength in front of frustrations, extracting things from others and condemned to suffer because life does not always quench our thirsts. When they refused, with an explanation, they proved their freedom and called us to be free, too, in our petition. So, we examined what we'd asked for and how we had asked. Likewise, with God, we can always petition, but we must clarify *what* we ask for and *how* we do it.

How to Petition

To ask for anything is connected with our dependence, and often we swing between too much independence and too much dependence. Sometimes we refuse any dependence; maybe because some people's answer to our petition was arbitrary, depending on their mood, according to their own interest or search for power. This hunger for independence explodes in those angry children who demand with exasperation, because they resent depending on others' will. Or, we limit our dependency by bargaining. "I'll do [I won't do] this if you give [if you don't give] me that." This blackmail keeps us independent in the measure we control the process. Impossible to play such games with God.

Or we are too dependent. Like children begging us to pick up a toy that is within their reach, we ask God to do everything, without accepting our own responsibility. "Give peace to my family, success for my exam," we pray, without contributing anything toward these ends. God wants our growth and cannot encourage such childish behavior. On the contrary, the Evil One always suggests to the child in us to tempt God (Mt 4:1–11; Lk 4:1–13).

So, *how* do we petition? Let us stay humble without servility and dignified without arrogance, for we are children of the God Jesus describes as the most loving Father. *Humility* makes us accept our fundamental poverty. Paul says, "What do you have that you did not receive?" David answers, Lord, "all things come from you" (1 Cor 4:7; 1 Chr 29:14). Teilhard de Chardin emphasized "the depth and universality of our dependence." Indeed, he found presumptuous to use the term *"my* life"* for the life that belongs ultimately to God. We are only the managers of God's gifts to us through others. Better to admit that, before life forces us to do so. Our dignity verifies our stewardship: Before asking God for anything, we must ask ourselves if we have done our part. All of this purifies our way of asking: Our prayer can no longer be that of passive and dependent babies or of arrogant and individualistic teenagers. God only desires us to become mature sons or daughters, as do parents who really work for the growth of their children. But how do we recognize that our petitions are made in a manner that honors who we are and who God is?

The Divine Milieu (New York: Harper & Row, 1960), pp. 76–77.

A Question of Freedom

Whatever our parents' answer to our petitions, we experienced their freedom. Maybe we were able to manipulate them sometimes; but this is impossible with God. God gives freely, and therefore invites us to be free, too — meaning, to dare to express freely our needs and to keep ourselves free before them.

Without bitterness, let us ask with the desire to respect God's freedom. "If Thy most Sacred Majesty should will to answer my plea," Ignatius of Loyola said. This is like the "please" we learn to say as children. But to say, "if it pleases you" is not humiliating to us when we have the humility and the dignity I described above. To ask and say "if you wish" is the prayer of adults who know that God-Love is still God. But recognizing God's freedom makes us free, too. For if we ask thus, we distance ourselves from our own petition and are prepared to see it not granted, at least not in the form we asked that it be. It might be painful as was the "Your will be done," of Jesus in his agony, but it is the price of our liberty (Lk 22:42). This means that we cherish, more than what we are asking for, our relationship with God, that love rooted in two freedoms as any love is.

Jesus guarantees the Father's gift if we ask "in his name." This is not to give lip service to his name at the end of a prayer, as some of the faithful do. It means to ask in reference to the whole of his being and personality, exactly as we aim at the whole person when we call someone. This is what we have just discovered: Like Jesus, we ask with the humility of the poor and the dignity of the responsible steward, as authentic sons or daughters and not as rebels or slaves. We don't pressure God, because our mutual relationship is too dear to our heart. If we want to behave as grown-up disciples of Jesus, this is wisdom — and the more so because *what* we are asking for is not as clear as we think.

"What Are You Looking For?"
(Jn 1:38)

Jesus says to James and John, and also to a blind man, "What is it you want me to do for you?" (Mk 10:36, 51; Mt 20:21; Lk 18:41). We anticipate and understand the answer of the disabled man; we are scandalized by the apostles'. Jesus accepts the two requests, and thus invites us to ask for what we want in our prayer. And, if we believe in a God who loves us infinitely, let us believe that what is best for us will be granted to us. But, is what is best for us *what* we are asking for? Do we even know what we are asking for?

Spontaneously, we reply, "Of course I want a job, a cure, a success, etc." After all, we always ask for serious things. But are they really what we most need for our growth? Children would say, "I want this toy, this ice cream." Spiritual authors recommend that we start praying by asking for the grace we desire. Which grace do we want, behind our immediate petition? Do we want a job or the social recognition that goes with it; our illness cured or not to remain inactive with the feeling of uselessness; a particular success or more dignity? For children, do they want a toy or to be equal to their peers, an ice cream or our attention? Examining our prayer shows that we always aim at *someone,* ourselves or somebody else, even when it seems that our prayer was aimed at *something.* Maybe Jesus thought so when he asked the first disciples, "*What* are you looking for?" even though they were following *him;* perhaps he wanted to make them discover their real search (Jn 1:38).

So, if like James and John, we don't know what we are asking for, we must be prudent with regard to a prayer that would be too specific (Mk 10:38). Let us ask but say, "God, I want this, but I am not sure it is the deepest desire of my being, so I let You determine the answer." Our freedom is then built into the prayer. We dare to ask with humility and dignity for what we are conscious about. But we stay free regarding our specific plea, and we accept God's absolute freedom, "for God is greater than our hearts" (1 Jn 3:20). However, I think that some specificity can still exist, not about the particular object of our prayer, but about some of its conditions or safeguards.

I would say, for instance, "God, I want a job, *but* first give me stamina to seek it; I ask for a cure, *but* give me patience during my sickness and consistency in taking medication; I pray for my success, *but* maintain me in humility." I believe that God acquiesces to the second part of our prayer. If James and John had petitioned for the grace of drinking Jesus' cup, the Father would not have needed an angel's help for the Son in agony. The two apostles would have been there, and awake (Lk 22:43). I believe that this kind of supplication co-incides with God's desire. In this case, John guarantees, "And this is the boldness we have in him, that if we ask anything according to his will, he hears us. And if we know that he hears us in whatever we ask, we know that we have obtained the requests made of him" (1 Jn 5:14–15).

Intercession

I have already written about intercession in the final pages of my book *God's Passion, Our Passion*. The practical goal of *this* book restricts me here to developing only *how* I think it is good to pray for others.

Intercession runs the same risks as any prayer made for ourselves. In it, we can be too independent or too dependent. We are arrogant if we think we can define what is best for others. We tempt God if we ask for a miracle without contributing our own efforts where we can. And we prepare pain for ourselves if we pray without freedom. And here again, *what* exactly do we ask for? Do we want peace for a country ravaged by war, or to get rid of news from there that disturbs our tranquillity, stirs up our guilt, aggravates our feeling of powerlessness? Do we want a cure for a friend or the end of our own worries, of our impatience, of our tiredness? Do we want the success of our children or to flatter our parental pride? Our intercessions are rarely unselfish. They need purification, as our prayers for ourselves also do.

Aware of this and hearing Jesus say, "Your Father knows what you need before you ask him," we could question, "So why would we intercede?" (Mt 6:8; Ps 139:4). Interceding is critical, as we realize that the Bible mentions twelve intercessions by Moses for Israel. We must plead for others because it is a source of marvelous blessings.

More than any other form of prayer, intercession forces us to confront whether or not we act for the ones we pray for (reminding us of the nonbelievers' remark, "Don't waste your time praying to someone in heaven. Do your work right now on earth!"). We must say with David, "I will not offer burnt offerings [here, let us include "prayers"] to the LORD my God that cost me nothing" (2 Sam 24:24).

Above all, by interceding we prove to ourselves that we care and love, with a heart like God's heart. Whoever forgets to intercede forgets to love. Intercession keeps the person we are praying for and God in our heart's memory, where we stay one with both. John affirms, "We have an advocate with the Father, Jesus Christ the righteous." So he says clearly that we are loved daily till the end of time, because Jesus keeps us in his heart (1 Jn 2:1). In the same way, the longer we implore, the more we discover *that our love for the person we are praying for has never been so present within ourselves.* And this is true not only of our love for those we pray for, but also of our love for God, as faith-ful: God's Name is at stake before all, in Bosnia-Herzegovina or Rwanda, in the action or the absence of the rich countries' believers; through wealthy suburban believers doing or not something for the poor of our cities. Confronted with suffering people, Jesus himself always did what he could, "so that they may believe" (Jn 11:42). Indeed, we can pray with the psalms and intercede for God's sake, "Rise up, O God, plead your cause; remember how the impious scoff at you all day long." But we must add, "Arise, O Love, within us. Defend your cause through us" (Ps 74).

This includes the sorrow, the patience, of waiting. If Mary prayed for her son Jesus during the Passion, she had to wait for days before his Resurrection, and for weeks before the coming of the Spirit of Love in the disciples' hearts. God's Spirit needed time to penetrate the inertia of matter and begin creation. Alas, our heart is often one of stone and takes its time to allow the Spirit of Love to act. Acknowledging that helps us not to condemn too hastily our leaders, who found a quick solution when Kuwait (a land with oil) was invaded by Iraq and delayed making a decision about Bosnia-Herzegovina or Rwanda (lands without oil). They are confronting their individual and our collective selfishness, the complexity of the problems, and many other things. It is the same at the local level (Ezek 36:26).

But the time of waiting and suffering is a purifying Passover, where we die to our frustrations, our preconceived ideas, our selfish needs, our definitions, our power and control, our idols, etc. We die *for* the sake of the other, the beloved we intercede for and our God. Intercession is, more than any other prayer, God's Paschal mystery within us. But *how* do we have to intercede?

How to Intercede

Aware of the issues raised above, we ask specifically for what is in our mind. We add what seems necessary for the other(s) *and* ourselves, *right now.* "God, give peace to Afghanistan, *but also* courage to those who suffer, to those trying to stop the conflict, and change the hearts of those who hate. *And* show me where are *my* prejudices." "God, deliver my mother from her torment, *but chiefly* give her light and patience in her plight. *And* help me to be your Son for her." "God, fix this marriage, *but* first give the spouses the grace of mutual listening, respect, and forgiveness. *And* show me how to help them best." "Ah, God, if my friend would not die! *But* liberate him from anguish, fill him with strength and peace. *And* give me the grace to love him more."

The freedom I spoke about then impregnates our intercession. Sure that God loves better than we do, we dare to ask for others what our heart wishes for them. But our distance from the specificity of our plea safeguards our freedom. Eventually, we entrust our loved one(s) into God's hands, compassion, and freedom — chiefly we do this when everything seems out of our power. Trusting, we enter into a mystery of which one element is the disposition of the person being prayed for (as an extreme example: What did God do with the heart of an insane Hitler or of a paranoid Stalin?).

However, the other things we freely ask for, like courage, conversion, light, patience, respect, pardon, strength and peace, are such God-like attributes that I believe they are granted, even though the mystery of another's relationship with God won't always make them visible to us (as an extreme example: When we pray for someone who is in coma, what is going on in and for him/her?). However, if we perceive the gigantic efforts made by many people for peace in countries at war, by many medical teams for a patient, by many educators for the maturing of children, by many volunteers for the elderly, the poor, or for prisoners, we already see and hear God's answer.

Finally, intercession drives us back to hope and faith. We have interceded for years for Northern Ireland, Timor, Haiti, Afghanistan, Cambodia. We have prayed for quite a while for the hungry children of our neighborhoods, for the victims of social injustice or discrimination. Or for a loved one who suffered and died. No good seems to have come. Indeed, we have seen the fall of many dictatorships, the end of apartheid in South Africa, the cure of our loved ones. But it took a while, and this erosion of time may have affected us. Do we *still* hope and believe in intercessory prayer, and also in the action of Love through so many dedicated men and women? Do we *still* hope and believe in a God of love who does all that is possible, in a Father who, Jesus would say, is no less torn apart than we might be, because his children are suffering?

I can now go to the related question, "Will God Grant My Prayer?" or "Does God Grant My Prayer?" in the next chapter.

Chapter 17

Will God Grant My Prayer?

NOW WE ARE ASKING, "Will God grant my prayer?" or, more often, "Why did God not grant my prayer?" We ask this with pain, anger, or, at least wonder. But our question and our feelings exist because, most of the time, we have not clarified if we could petition for everything, and if we know what and how to ask.

Granted According to God's Desire

Asking as I have described in the preceding chapter might eliminate our questions. If we admit that we never know perfectly what we want deep down within ourselves, the question might already become "null and void," as a judge would decree. Indeed, Jesus asserts, "Ask, and it will be given you; search, and you will find; knock, and the door will be opened for you" (Mt 7:7). But he does not say that we would receive *exactly* what we asked for, find *exactly* what we sought, and that the door opened to us would be *exactly* the one we knocked at. In John's Gospel, Jesus always answers questions, but rarely the way they are asked, like Isaiah's God, who said, "My thoughts are not your thoughts" (Isa 55:8). Therefore, if we believe that God always hears "when the afflicted ones call out," let us believe also that our requests are granted one way or *another* (Ps 34:7).

We must look at the balance sheet of petitions made according to the above suggestions. We have asked in accord with a specific need, ours or (it seems) another's. But we have enlarged our plea to include graces certainly necessary for us and others, like strength, courage, patience. We have also taken our responsibility and acted (once more or finally). We have remained open to receive God's other answers, and we have already seen them in part in the situation (e.g., people working for peace, against discrimination). We have accepted purification and conversion within ourselves and in our relationship with others and with God, with whom we are more united than ever. We have accepted time and suffering in the process, with more mature and renewed hope and faith.

With so many graces, *will we still say that our prayers have not been granted,* for what concerns ourselves? Concerning those we interceded for, all of this is still true, but marked by the mystery of their own being and of their relationship with God. We see this mystery in God granting the demands of Gideon, who was not too courageous, the unexpected contrite and humble prayer of Ahaz, the request of Jonah who had run away from his mission, and even the plea of the murderer Cain (Judg 6; 1 Kings 21; Jon 2; Gen 4).

Martha is a model when she said to Jesus, "Lord, if you had been here, my brother would not have died. But even now I know that God will give you whatever you ask of him" (Jn 11:21–22). Freely, she dares to express her specified desire (with a bit of sad and loving reproach?). But she also asserts freely her faith and her openness to a "whatever" defined by Jesus and his God only. The answer goes beyond the expectation! God does the same with us, when we know better what to ask for and how to ask for it.

More recent than Martha's, here are two examples that taught me a lot:

- A young man has been paralyzed for months. Daily, teenagers visit him. It happens that a young priest joins the group. A few months later, before the group, this priest all of a sudden commands the patient, "In Jesus' name, get up and walk!" No result! The witness who told me the story was saddened by the event. What was in the priest's mind? He did not find God's presence where it was obvious and looked for it elsewhere. I wonder what happened then to the teenagers' faith and to the *miracle* of their daily visits?

- I met Bill during retreats in prison. Often, I saw him in town, after his prison term was over. This tough man used to talk about prostitutes and French history, but, each time, he gave me a pearl in the midst of his sordid subject matter. One day, he said, "When I pray [guess my surprise!], I say to God — Hi, God! Thank you for what you have given me and my son today. Please take care of both of us tomorrow. Already thank you for what you are going to do. But I won't bother you much longer. You have so much to do for people needier than me. So, good night." Wow!

For Our Children

Our treatment of any request from our children educates them for their prayer of petition. If we allow them to be insatiable dictators getting everything from us, their reactions in front of an absolutely free God are predictable. If we refuse too often with anger and no serious explanation, how will they deal with a God able to choose many other solutions than ours?

Let us hypothesize that our children are being raised well. Teaching them how to ask God for something starts each time we help them to reflect about what they want, for example with what they learned through past experiences: "Remember, you wanted badly this white toy truck, but after a few hours you were no longer playing with it." "Have you forgotten? We bought the bike you wanted. Three days later, it no longer interested you. Sorry, but the money spent for it is no longer available." Children can understand such explanations. Vincent, seven years old, has bought five small toy cars with his allowance, and he says to me, "There was a superb race car! But if I had bought it, I would not have been able to buy any other cars." My little neighbors ask me for candies; I always invite them to make a choice, after a (short) moment of reflection, "Tootsie Rolls, Almond Joys, Bazooka gum, M & Ms, Now and Afters? Take your time and tell me what you want." We must prevent ourselves from inviting our children to ask God for trivial things. Better to train them in maturity and freedom, which will be so useful in the world, and also, of course, each time they are going to pray to God for something they want. However, even with this kind of intelligent upbringing, I think it necessary to say to children, "Do not be afraid to ask God for what you want," in order to establish, and *first of all,* their total freedom with God. Then it is up to them to manage their petitions to God in the privacy of their heart.

If we have to teach a group of children, it is important to give them the same sort of formation. When I had to do that, the most difficult part was to make them aware of God's freedom because of the ways their parents misused their own freedom. So I did not instruct them to use the phrase "if you wish" in their prayers. I wanted to prevent any confusion with the "please" they had learned (not always in the most desirable circumstances) to use socially. I have always made this distinction with my little neighbors: "I love you enough not to be too concerned if you say 'please' or 'thank you' to me or not. But I will sometimes remind you of these words, because it is necessary to be polite with others. I would be sad if people thought bad things about you." I don't want the relationship with God-Love to be reduced to the level of social behaviors, as good as they might be.

It seems to me essential to teach intercession to children, for it forces them out of their tendency to be self-centered and to ask for themselves only. As I have already said, it is preparing their heart to embrace the world as God's heart does. So, when the opportunity is given us, we intercede with them for suffering people in our family or neighborhood: Aunt Mary is sick, Joseph broke his leg. We do the same for those in pain, far from us (in fact, television makes everything close today, although, for children's minds, it mixes reality and fiction, changes violence and sorrow into commonplace and quickly forgotten shows). But if we intercede with children, it is only once in a while, in order not to burden their hearts.

In the primary school, we sometimes petitioned for others in liturgies. We asked for patience for a student or a teacher who was sick, or for courage for people suffering from a war or a flood. We always asserted that God liked such a prayer and was already at work. To demonstrate this last point, we always emphasized those struggling for peace, for a cure or a reconciliation, and we never hid from the children that life was often a battle. And we gave thanks for the men and women who devoted themselves to causes like peace or justice in troubled parts of the world.

In order to avoid children's possible future disappointments, we proceeded sometimes as we did for prayer about our sins: using little stories (see Chapter 11, "Must I Pray about My Sins?"). We evoked memories: "It took a while for *us* to be able to forgive our friend. In the country we're discussing, people have fought one another for years. So God is working in everybody's heart there, but it will take time before we see a success." "We remember, our cold or our flu was not cured immediately. So it will take time for God to be able to work through doctors, nurses, and medication, and heal those we know who are ill." "We did what we could for our hamster or our turtle. But it died. Death exists, and people are dying everyday. But God helps those we know and those who are dying to be at peace, our Grandpa or Grandma or somebody else."

We may also help children reflect about our own actions. "Yes, in that country people are at war. But it started like some of our fights here. What can we do to keep or to reestablish peace among us?" "We have prayed for George who is sick. What could we do for him? Shall we all sign a card, write a collective letter, send drawings?" These suggestions utilized their compassion to motivate them to act in a responsible way and according to their capabilities.

And, eventually, we entrusted all those we had prayed for to Jesus, "who will take, comfort and keep them in his arms, as a mother, a father, a friend, a nurse, does with us when we hurt and are very sick." We were right to say that, for the God of Hosea asserts, "I took them up in my arms. . . . I led them with cords of human kindness, with bands of love. I was to them like those who lift infants to their cheeks" (Hos 11:3–4).

Chapter 18

What Is the Use of Praise?

T HE FIRST PURPOSE of Christian liturgy is to give thanks and praise. Therefore it says how important praise is. So, eventually, our heart must praise, too, in a personal way. The question posed by this chapter often takes two different forms. One is expressed by people who value effectiveness and are irritated by some Christians who praise too glibly. The other comes from people who, in good faith, ask about praise because they think it is not easy to practice. This story could answer both groups: Tony, seven years old, opens a splendid birthday present, which he has long desired. After a short moment of amazement, he claps his hands, directing his applause *at his parents,* and shouts, "Bravo!" That shows almost everything there is about praise. But then, why is this chapter near the end of the book? The reason is that, in my opinion, authentic praise is possible only after many experiences described in the preceding pages have been known (and that was not in Tony's praise; hence I wrote "almost.") Let me explain my point.

Some Praise Is Too Easy

Some Christians aggravate us because they seem to praise God too facilely. Is their prayer empty words, never tested by fire? If we ignore the suffering of the world and do nothing

129

about it, how can we praise God with realism and honesty? Do we praise seriously if we have not agonized, prayed, and discerned about our sins, and experienced contrition and forgiveness? What is the value of our praise if work or sickness have never burdened us? Finally, it is only after having been purified in our demands and crucified in our intercessions that we can praise God without fickleness. Many psalms prove that, but I'll mention only two biblical prayers of praise. The longest one was sung by Shadrak, Meshak, and Abednego, but *in a furnace,* where they were supposed to die because they refused idolatry (Dan 3:51–90). Job prays the shortest one: "The LORD gave, and the LORD has taken away; blessed be the name of the LORD!" after *he has lost everything* (Job 1:21). And one of the most famous Christian works of praise, the Canticle of Creatures, was composed by Francis of Assisi, after many misadventures and not too long before he died (indeed, he praises God "for our sister *death* no human being can escape," but without direct explanation). Praise that does not encompass what we have passed through is too easy and does not honor either ourselves or God. The prayer of praise that has been put to the test is beautiful, but never easy. Of course, our praise will be perfect in heaven when we are with the cherubim and the twenty-four elders, but we can start to practice it on earth (Isa 6; Rev 4). It is possible to distinguish two different steps in praise.

From the Gifts to the Giver, and Beyond

Praise is often directly linked with thanksgiving. We, or others, have been liberated from some suffering or forgiven, we have savored success and grace, we have been gifted generously. So, gratefully, we turn ourselves toward the One who has given so much. Tony shouting "Bravo!" expressed his gratitude to his parents. We do the same, saying, "God, I thank and praise you for what you have granted."

This praise is beautiful, but still centered on ourselves, for its logic is, "I praise You for what You did *for me, or others*" (this implies a risk: no gift, no praise!). So, here, praise reaches God by bouncing back. And, somehow, it is easy, because it has already been rewarded in advance by God. Then, sometimes, we still say, "Thank you for your gift," but *we add something about the giver.* "Joe pulled me out of my ordeal; *he is great!* Anne forgave me; *what a big heart* !" That is exactly what struck me in Tony's praise: He directed his clapping *at* his parents, not at the present or at himself.

In front of the benefit, a shift is made toward another mode of praise. Still there subsists some bond with the received grace, but a distance takes place between the gift and the praise following it. We "forget" the favor and ourselves, and we no longer say, "You are great *because . . .*" We exult for God, and God only: "Wow!" We are *in ecstasy* before this surprising Being revealed through the Giver. In Latin, ecstasy means to stand out, out of oneself. We are *out* of ourselves and look at God only. Such a move out of ourselves is not always easy, because it is rarely spontaneous for us.

Our praise then treats God as God. We marvel before Someone, perceived now as extra-ordinary, as perfectly Other, as a transcendent Love far beyond all experiences or hopes, imaginations or desires. We are engulfed in astonishment and surprise, amazement and stupefaction, wonder and admiration, rapture and awe, even a kind of incredulity: "It's impossible, not true! I cannot believe it! It's too much! *You* are too much!" It is like when we meet a very exceptional woman or man, when we hear an extraordinary voice or enjoy an unbelievably delicious dish. It was my experience, after having for the first time heard Mahler's Ninth Symphony directed by Bernstein and seen Magritte's painting "The Dominion of Light." We are in front of a "too much" so big that everything else takes its real place, the back seat. This "too much" Love we experience as our God.

An Extraordinary and Ordinary Beyond

After having walked for hours on a cold night, when we arrive at the peak for sunset, it is there, there only, that ecstasy
is soaring. In order to praise accurately, we must have known
the apprenticeship of life and faith (it is not a question of
age, because some young people can live spiritually in the fast
lane). Through ups and downs, we must accept the patient
training of our capacity to see God acting in human deeds.

We would be blind if we could not see and praise God in
heroic situations. I read in the newspapers on July 7, 1994,
"Man's CPR skills save three victims of a lightning bolt."
Recently, thirteen firefighters, including two women, struggling for the sake of property and people, died in a forest fire
in California. "Wow, God, you are admirable!" I said when
I heard about the driver who risked his life and drove his
truck in flames away from homes. "Wow, God, you are incredible!" I exulted when I saw a man hugging in court the
mothers of the teenagers who tried to burn him alive. Indeed,
there, an extra-ordinary God-Love is visible and deserves our
praise.

Is it less easy to see God in a tragedy? Two of my friends,
mentioned in *God's Passion, Our Passion,* died. After years
of suffering, she passed away on Tuesday; he died Wednesday; both were in their thirties. That was sad, but what a
wonderful love between them and their people. The war in
Bosnia-Herzegovina goes on and on, but so does the tenacity
of those fighting for peace. One hundred thousand soldiers,
trained for war, are working under the UN in 1994 for peace
in more than fifteen places in the world; we have never seen
that, though Isaiah had said, "They shall beat their swords
into plowshares, and their spears into pruning hooks" (2:4).
What can we say in the face of all the volunteers risking their
lives in starving South Sudan or torn-apart Rwanda, or elsewhere? Nothing but, "O Lord, our Sovereign, how majestic
is your name in all the earth!," or just, "Wow, God-Love, you
are too much!" (Ps 8:1).

But we can see God in simpler events; Nazareth was ordinary for Jesus. A man waters the plants of a neighbor who is hospitalized, a woman runs errands for a pregnant friend, a child shovels the snow in the driveway of old people for no payment, an obliging operator gives us the needed information, a mail deliverer says with her heart, "Have a good day!" Are not these persons permeated by Someone who deserves praise? "Wow, God, really, who are you?" is what I think when I give Christ's Body to little children in church.

The mystery of God-Love, endlessly acting through us, provokes our praise. "You are fantastic, there in the most terrible or commonplace circumstances of our life!" *But that supposes that we are able to see!* Praising challenges us. According to the practical goal of this book, let us pray often with the question, "Where, around me or in the news, *have I seen God-Love today?*" I hope we'll find reasons to praise God. Each time we see God in our life, the Covenant is renewed, of which Deuteronomy says, "But take care and watch yourselves closely, so as neither to forget the things that your eyes have seen nor to let them slip from your mind all the days of your life," and for our current events, as long as we don't fall asleep (Deut 4:9). "It is good...to declare your steadfast love in the morning, and your faithfulness by night" (Ps 92:1–2).

What Is the Use?

The things said above help us now to answer the question, "What's the use of *formal* praise?" I could mention customs common to all religions, monks and their daily office, the Eucharist; and I could assert that praising individually is good. To quote Ireneus of Lyon, "The Glory of God is the human person fully alive." Yes, God is glorified in any man or woman who gives freedom of action to the Love within themselves. In that sense, God does not need our formal praise. Of course, formal praise must also be avoided if its purpose is to revere a superior, a "Lord," as a fearful courtesan does ("Let us praise God, for we never know."). So, then, what can formal praise do for us, for God?

Linked to a grace, it best expresses our gratitude. And when it surpasses the gift and the thank you, the other and ourselves, and is ecstatic before that Love "out of this world" but experienced here and now, it fulfills the Law, the Psalms, and the Prophets. Without ignoring the other commandments, it puts *the first back in first place,* "The LORD is our God, the LORD alone! You shall love the LORD your God with all your heart, and with all your soul, and with all your might" (Deut 6:5, Mk 12:29). Both God and we ourselves are dignified, as a Braque and a Picasso were when each one saw himself admired in his paintings by the other. Again, it is important for us to verify often if we praise this way.

After all, we say, "Hallowed be thy Name," meaning: May your Name, your Being as Love, be honored and praised (and we insist: "Love, may thy kingdom come, thy will be done on earth as it is in heaven."). So let us start to do it, individually. What is the use of it? Nothing, I would say to people fond of efficiency, since it is all ecstatic, all gratuitous: We don't try to get something, we just admire; that's it. No, it is more than that. I doubt that praising is useless, if we look at love. Pure love means to say, without ulterior motives, to my wife or my daughter, "You are beautiful!" It is gratuitous because it is totally other-centered, but it expresses and effectively feeds love. Even God does that! God, the Bridegroom, said to the Bride, Israel or the Church, humankind or each one of us, "Ah, you are beautiful, my beloved, ah, you are beautiful!" Is it useless to hear God saying that to us throughout so many verses, during our whole life? So, why would we not reply, formally, like the Bride, "My lover is radiant and ruddy.... His head is pure gold.... His eyes are like doves beside running waters" (Song 4; 5)? Does it do nothing for us to be ecstatic before the beauties of God, in the face of Love — when God is the most marvelous piece of art? My wife or my daughter is touched when I magnify her beauty; God, who deserves it more, is also touched when we praise.

I think of the Down syndrome child I mentioned earlier, who repeated intensely for weeks as his evening prayer, "God is great!" Psalms had already said, "May all who seek you rejoice and be glad in you; may those who love your salvation say continually, 'Great is the LORD!'" and "Out of the mouths of babes and infants you have fashioned praise" (Ps 40:16; 8:2). Yes, "I thank you, Father, Lord of heaven and earth, because you have hidden these things from the wise and the intelligent and have revealed them to infants" (Lk 10:21).

For Our Children

It is important to educate children about praise, for authentic praise is not always provided by society. Praises can be too lavish: Just listen to the superlatives and comparatives distributed indiscriminately in any award ceremony. Or praise can be given badly: Just listen carefully to many commercials. And often, what does it praise?

The first school of praise is family, where our children must hear us praise intelligently, so that we "tell the next generation that this is God" (Ps 48:13–14). Any openness to the esthetic enters into this purpose, and it is a joy to see parents initiating children to beauty in a museum.

Some people use nature for teaching children to praise God. We all have been touched by a sunset, the moon playing with clouds, a chain of mountains covered with snow. But how do we apply that to God with children? Jesus never praises God with nature; if he mentions nature, it is always to send people back to the understanding of the Kingdom or a more fruitful faith. Also, very few psalms directly use nature for praising God. They most often see in it an order according to God's precepts (the Law?), or a proof of God's power for Israel's and humankind's benefit. And in the psalms where we find praise, it is connected with a grace for an individual or God's People. All of this invites us to be prudent and intelligent when we use nature, if we don't want to land at two impasses. Our praise may be a pagan one, aiming at a Creator rather indifferent to human beings, without Covenant and Jesus. Or it is a praise to a god synonymous with life, in which the little and weak creatures are victims of the jungle law, which is not especially evangelical.

That is why, in the school, when we used nature for the praise of God, we proceeded in the following way. What we said was always connected with human history and Jesus' God. An extreme example is Psalm 29, where God is praised in a storm that "breaks the cedars of Lebanon," which we never take as such, for children are scared by storms (also, what kind of God is behind that?). How can we praise God in floods or tornadoes, earthquakes or hurricanes, destroying everything, killing people, and depicted on television. When we had to pray about cataclysms, we praised the rescuers' courage, the victims' mutual aid, and the gifts of so many others. So we used nature to recall the signs of the Kingdom, to magnify the fruitfulness of faith in Love through a lot of women and men. And we invited the children to be in ecstasy in front of Jesus' Spirit, the Spirit of Love acting in human history, and to pray that we would let Love act in the same way through us. We followed the same logic as we do with news about tragedies created by human beings, like wars.

Once a year, we had a liturgy centered on Creation (Gen 1). We insisted on what is beautiful, but chiefly on love. We emphasized that everything was a gift from an extraordinary beautiful Love. A Love who took our flesh in Jesus and made us in his own image and likeness as loving beings, through the Spirit of Love within us. This led us to praise and to ask ourselves, "If we love God and others, how could we become vandals, and what can we create for others' joy?" Our logic was: to see Love working through us, in any event, act of nature, or human beings, good or bad (thus, terrible occurrences were never forgotten). And finally we praised God: "You are fantastic!" This finale always found an echo in children's hearts, while they were invited to be in ecstasy before persons other than themselves; for everybody knows how much children are touched when we say to them, "You are fantastic!"

NOTE: When no children in the group were afflicted by any physical infirmity, the Olympic Games or some other big sports event gave us the opportunity to praise God for the marvelous gift of our body. A videocassette allowed us to admire the flexibility, the beauty, and the potential prowess of a human body that was well taken care of and trained. We then remembered that God loved the human body to the point of taking one in Jesus. And we gave thanks and praise for Jesus, so close to us incarnate beings.

Chapter 19

How Can We Pray,
As a Family, As Spouses?

THE QUESTION is often asked with a sense of powerlessness. Many parents want to pray with their children, as a family. But they don't know what to do, either because that habit did not exist in their childhood or because they have only bad memories of it. Reciting the same grace before meals when you are hungry, or the same verbal prayers while kneeling on the floor when you want to sleep, with no permission to refuse to do so, has rarely been very attractive to children. So it's no surprise if later, when children subjected to such coerced prayers have become parents, praying as a family is a problem.

However, I won't deny too quickly the value of the customs I mentioned. One reason is that we never know their real impact on children. One day, a friend of mine, a Jesuit priest, told me, "I cannot fall asleep without saying the Our Father. For I have always in my mind the picture of my father, saying this prayer with deep conviction, with one knee on a chair just behind us. I cannot say that I was fond of that family prayer, but something there was powerful for me." So it won't hurt to pray as a family if we allow some freedom and creativity. To pray too often and too mechanically may damage the value of what we do, may tire and disgust our children. Also, they may think that "reciting" is sufficient, and their prayer life will perhaps never move beyond that. Here is an example of family prayer I was often part of.

A Scriptural Liturgy
Prepared and Performed by Children

I'll call them the Smiths, a couple and five children (two young teenagers and a set of triplets around ten years old). Obviously, they knew how to pray in an interesting way, for, as soon as one of them would suggest a family prayer for someday later, all agreed. The children would decide who would select a text from the gospel (often, the one of a following Sunday), or some songs or some specific intentions, etc.

When the day of our rendezvous with God came, we would go to the living room, all of us except anyone who decided not to join the group, for freedom was the first rule. Freedom was also visible in our bodily postures: One was in a comfortable chair, another lying or sitting down on the carpet, another standing up nearby the fireplace or prostrate in a corner. I never heard any comment about that. Then, according to their self-assigned tasks, the children were taking charge of everything. They had already prepared books, lights, music, an icon, etc. After the reading of the gospel by one of them, we would stay silent for a short while. Then we would share about the text, answering the question "What touched you the most in this story? And if you want to, tell us why." Nobody was forced to share. Sharing would often open a kind of discussion among all of us. Anyone's word was welcomed with the same attention; I still remember the insightful remarks of the ten-year-old son. Then, whoever wanted to would offer to the group their intentions concerning relatives, school, friends, current national or international news. And we would pray for those intentions either silently or with the same repeated invocation. Here or there, some songs were sung. The concluding prayer was always the Lord's Prayer, said aloud by all of us.

I named this family prayer "liturgy," for it was one, lasting sometimes an hour and a half. And the ministers were the children themselves. I never heard one of them complain about those liturgies; on the contrary, many things read, said, or heard that evening would generate conversations during the following days. And the family's guests, children or adults like me, present by chance that evening, were always very impressed by the whole liturgy, because we were all fed by one another in terms of information about prayer, spiritual sensitivities, Scriptures, and God.

This is just an example, but it has been for me the proof that it is possible and easy to pray as a family, if we know how to excite and call the creativity of our children and use our own. The family prayer of my Jesuit friend had an impact on him in spite of all its defects. So, we can guess the influence on children of a liturgy like the Smiths'.

Spouses Who Pray Together

The minimum conjugal prayer life seems to be to say together aloud some verbal prayer. But the structure of the Smiths' family prayer shows that we can go further. Spouses can also sing songs, read Scripture, stay silent for a while, and share their intentions of the day. For people who are used to formal personal prayer, the moment of silence might be long. I think of spouses praying silently at the beach, during vacation.

Some others practiced this variant: They prayed together each day, briefly, saying the Our Father, for example. But they arranged a rendezvous in prayer for some later date, and they decided the content of it. They selected a passage of Scripture, or the readings of the coming liturgy, deciding that they would pray individually on it during the days before their encounter. The rendezvous was essentially a time for sharing about their personal prayer with the selected texts, following, for instance, the three points "What? How? Why?" described in Chapter 8, "Do I Have to Keep a Journal?"

Some people would say that such sharing is not praying. However, most of the best spiritual masters of the past have viewed this kind of conversation as so nourishing that they equated it to a fruitful prayer. And last but not least, this sharing of spiritual information is a wonderful way for spouses to grow deeper in their mutual knowledge, in their individual and common spiritual journey with God, in their love and in Love, all fruit of what is called prayer. To "date" each other in God's company, is that not a marvelous prayer? It is the repetition of a song of songs between spouses that is a sacrament of the Song of Songs of the Bride and the Bridegroom.

I need not emphasize the fact that what has been suggested for spouses can be done by friends as well.

Chapter 20

How Can God
Become Real for Me?

MY ANSWER TO THE QUESTION could simply be, "*Practice* the content of this book, and God will become real for you," for I've seen it happening for most of the people I have helped. Only three persons discovered one day that they were not, in fact, Christians or believers; but their honest attempt freed them from useless questions and sent them back to live according to the value system they believed in. But I would like to explain briefly some stages of prayer life experienced by those for whom God became real. This will save readers from surprises in their own journey and help them to understand the evolution of their relationship with God. What follows is a summary of the experiences of persons I have known, as well as my own.

What do people mean when they say, "One day, God became real for me"? Two stories can explain this. At Ellen and Robert's wedding, the celebrant explained the choice of the two readings, a text of Erich Fromm and one of John the evangelist: "Both Ellen and Robert believe in Love, but for her Love is a Person." Also, during a workshop about prayer, some people said, "I felt God present and saying to me..." or "God touched me through this verse..." or "I experienced God's love for me...." And they explained, "I felt a profound peace invading me; I was touched to tears by the verse; My heart was full of some sort of warmth." All spoke about *emotions they had felt*. "Ah," said a man who was clearly less religious, "I have known such emotions, but I don't call them God's presence." We all understood then that the persons who "experienced" God used phrases describing feelings they had experienced *and* decoded according to their faith.

So, when people say that God became real for them, it is usually because they have experienced some enlivening feelings, while praying, for instance. And because they believe that God's Spirit dwells within themselves, they interpret these emotions as signals of God's presence. For them, *God was felt* as real (for more on this, see Chapter 7, "How Can I Decode What Is Going On in My Prayer?"). Furthermore, these experiences often created changes of behavior in them, let us say *conversions*. The process seems to have taken the following three steps.

From Milk to Meat

1. The beginning is like a honeymoon. Praying is easy because many things happen during prayer. The intellect makes discoveries. Consolations (or desolations) abound, and are sometimes powerful ("orgasms" or "surgeries," a friend of mine used to call such feelings). Spiritual authors say that God spoils us, as parents do children. Some psychologists say that old inner wounds are revealed, and somehow partly or totally healed. Believers attribute this action to God's Spirit in themselves. Everyone speaks the language of his or her culture.

2. Then the intellect reflects less. Consolations are fewer but deeper (and more similar to "intellectual consolations," described in Chapter 7). The process is a succession of longer and longer *plateaus,* interrupted by *flights* (or deepenings within oneself). Some psychologists say that a harmony develops and allows deeper discoveries. God no longer feeds us with milk but with meat, as Paul's words

remind us: "I fed you with milk, not solid food, for you were not ready for solid food" (1 Cor 3:2).

3. Finally, prayer life most of the time becomes a plateau; peaks and valleys are the exception. The intellect is at rest. Consolations are rare, very short but sharp, and occur anywhere and about anything; someone told me, "They are God's twinklings of an eye." The authors say that spiritual sensuality and superficiality have quieted down. Some psychologists would say that we are at last at peace with our unconscious. The relationship with God is characterized by more and more *serenity and contentment*. It seems sometimes that nothing is happening, except when an exceptional shock hits our life. Even though we can still sometimes be disturbed, we are not easily deeply destroyed.

All through the process, feelings increase faith, and faith helps raise the tide of feelings. We experience the same in the course of a love affair. But we must remember Moses' lesson: Usually, we become conscious of the change *afterward,* for God is seen only from the back (Ex 33:23). So, during the passage from one step to another, we might feel lost, for our past landmarks no longer work, and our God takes on new features. It is advisable to have a good spiritual helper on hand. Behind this process, which requires years of regular practice of prayer, some trends appear, all showing a "more and more" tendency.

More and More Freedom

Those for whom God is real don't feel frustrated when intellectual or emotional gratifications become rare, although it is not easy to persist in formal prayer without rewards. Here, again, a spiritual helper is valuable. Those who persevere are increasingly detached concerning God's "treats." Knowing that a peak experience does not last, they accept with peace and patience the preparation necessary for another spiritual flight. For they no longer treat God as the supplier of their needs. They desire but never pressure God. If their prayer is austere and "gently boring," they make it even more a gratuitous offering. "I am here for You, do what You want. You are my Host, I accept your menu."

Body, journal, methods, are managed more freely. These people hear their body and find the posture that fits the moment and place. They analyze themselves less through a journal, except for times of crisis or important discernment. They have grown through practicing methods, and they know which one fits a specific situation, like virtuosos improvising with talent because they have practiced for years. They are even freer about information that is less necessary, because they have sufficient knowledge about themselves and their God; exactly as we need less to look at signs along a road we have followed a thousand times. "I know enough about me, You, what we can do together. I know You are acting, so I do my part, *what I can*."

This last point is obvious in the way those for whom God has become real manage their distractions or sins. They smile at the creations of their imagination, as we do at a boisterous child's inventions, without losing sight of their inner Host. They decode easily the distractions' meaning, as well as they do their devils' language. They understand the saying "The closer God is, the more all hell breaks loose." So they are not surprised by the mechanism and subtlety of their temptations, and are more concerned by those hidden in overzealous dedication than those rooted in human weaknesses. A more compassionate attitude toward themselves as sinners has developed deeper because they know well the language of Jesus' God, now real for them: "I desire mercy, not sacrifice" (Mt 9:13). But they do what they can to fulfill God's desire: "Have I any pleasure in the death of the wicked, says the Lord GOD, and not rather that they should turn from their ways and live?" (Ezek 18:23). They have even accepted in peace that some areas in themselves remain obscure, because

they know God is present there. They just go back to the Father who is keeping vigil for them, as the sons or daughters
they are, for their stage makeup is gone (Lk 15.) "I know, I'll
always limp, but I can still walk toward your banquet where
You want me" (Lk 22:1–14).

Even more, they have seen God's grace acting through
their faults; as someone said to me, "I thank God for my
doubts; they allow me to help people afflicted by such temptations." I understood this at the fiftieth wedding-anniversary
celebration of old friends. At the moment of toasting, the
wife stood up and said things so surprising that her husband
left the table, furious. The oldest son reproached her, "Mom,
why did you ruin our festivity by saying that?" Her reply
stunned us: "You don't know him. I do. The party would not
have been complete if I had not given him the joy of his little
daily outburst!" When the old man came back, all smiles, we
knew that she had been right.

More and More All the Time

When God becomes real for us, we "think" of God all the
time. It is not a conscious thought, but something like when
my wife works at her computer on one floor of our home
and I am loading the washing machine on another; our attention focuses on what we do, but we are aware of each
other's presence, because love is there. This awareness comes
from the fact that leaving the world for formal prayer is not
forgetting human beings, and leaving prayer for the world is
never putting God aside. News and Good News both speak
about God-Love. This increases freedom concerning formal
prayer times, their preparation and length, or the use of
Scripture. The preparation is simpler, for almost any text says
something about God's presence in human events. To stay
a shorter or longer time is no longer too important, for the
connection with God is real anywhere and at any time, be
it formal or not. News and Scriptures are both God's Word,

and switching from one to the other is not switching; although the persons I am talking about stay attached to the Bible as the best tool to decode human history and their own. They are just sorry, with no guilt, when they can't find time to pray formally with Scripture, as Pierre and Mary were when they could not give priority to their mutual love (see Chapter 14, "How Can I Pray When I Am Too Busy?"). As soon as possible, they go back to God's Word.

Finally, such awareness about Love's active presence produces permanent praise. However, it does not deny what is wrong in and around us, because God's action is not always welcomed by human beings. So people for whom God is real are inclined to do what they can for Love.

More and More Disposed to Act

Many famous Christian mystics were very active people. Dedicated to do "nothing" in prayer, they were the most impelled to act in the world. It was not an escape from God, but a zeal born in prayer. They could not ignore their words, "Love, thy will be done on earth as it is in heaven," or John's: "Those who do not love a brother or sister whom they have seen, cannot love God whom they have not seen" (1 Jn 4:20). They knew that a good tree gives good fruit (Mt 7:16–20). They probably thought, as a French poet said, "My God, the more I eat You, the more You become my instinct." So, loving Love, they wanted to work for God, who was so real for them in human history, whether hurting or winning.

I see that in people for whom God has become real. Able to decode God's message through Scripture or news, they know more accurately what they can or cannot do. They know their peculiar needs or nature: more contemplative or more active; loners or team people; leaders or followers; but all freely and responsibly do their task, no more no less. They "love, not in word or speech, but in truth and action" (1 Jn 3:18). They may act because of ethical, philosophical, or political reasons, but their deepest motive is to act for God's sake, for Love's chance here and now. Penance is included in their action when, for instance, they restrain themselves to be a part of orientations, attitudes, behaviors, that are far from Jesus' message of love: I think of a friend of mine who refuses to partake of any joke concerning women or homosexuals. They all practice the humble and fruitful daily pledge of another friend of mine, "God, I promise to you that I'll try to love everybody I meet today." So, these people, free from any comparison with people who can do a lot, act with the power they have, although they suffer to be unable to do even more. They don't envy "heroes"; they just abandon themselves to Love's power. They know that the universality of Love always takes place in the particular action they do here and now, and that, eventually, they can always supplicate.

When they do it, they follow what I said about asking for something or somebody. But they ask less and less for themselves, sure that "God provides," like patients who know that the nurse watches over them (Gen 22:14). But they become bolder and bolder, more than Abraham, in their intercession for others, believing Jesus' words, "Will not God grant justice to his chosen ones who cry to him day and night?" (Gen 18:16–33; Lk 18:7). For the reasons I have explained, they "fight" lovingly with the God who is real for them, as Mary did with Jesus in Cana (Jn 2:1–12). They do so because asking God for accountability honors the One they pray to, just as they are honored when God does the same with them. Not "fighting" would imply that they don't trust God's capacity and will to extract a resurrection from any cross. Many verses of the psalms justify that boldness (e.g., Ps 13:2).

Their last reason: to comfort God's heart. They are sure that God, hearing their intercession, rejoices with a sigh of gratitude: "Thanks a lot, I was afraid to be the only one aching because of children with no food in Rwanda or the United States, because of violence in democracies or in Bosnia-Herzegovina, because of racism everywhere!" With a retreatant, we pictured Jesus talking with friends about football at the wedding in Cana, and a little annoyed by Mary's request. But we imagined the mutual grateful smile mother and son shared in the car while driving back home and saying, "Fantastic, we did it!"

"You did it through me, through them! You are fantastic!" is increasingly the heart's refrain of people for whom God is real. They do not exult because Jupiter is hit by the fragments of the Shoemaker-Levy comet, but because they see more and more clearly Jesus' God in all human events, as real as any human being. Jesus was even able to discern in a dishonest wily manager an example for the sons of light (Lk 16:1–8). Similarly, a friend of mine said to me, "Ah, if we only had the same creativity and dedication, tenacity and boldness, for the poor as some lawyers have for the sake of a hero in sports, music, athletics, or politics!" People for whom God has become real are more and more in awe before the mystery of God's real presence.

More and More Certain, Less and Less Sure

The journey of those for whom God has become real deepens their faith. Their prayer is simpler and simpler, and they don't worry if it is easy or not, fervent or dry, spectacular or banal. They know that they'll always somehow be deaf to God's word, but they are more and more certain that God is there, as a kind of elusive presence, similar to my wife's for me and mine for her when we work silently on two different floors. And, more and more, silence takes over.

The seekers were first just unaware of their own spiritual depth, but when God became real for them, they discovered that they had an "inner life." It was like a founding event: Everything was already said by God there, but not yet totally unfolded for them. So, they were for a while arrested by their discoveries about themselves, through many thoughts, images, and words. Then they realized slowly that Someone was lovingly pointing out all of that in them, as a guest would advise us tactfully about the refined or vulgar decorations of our home. Later, focusing less on themselves, they were more and more captivated by the astonishing Spirit of Love in themselves. Finally, they just stayed more and more silently "passive," gaping at all the potential Love in them, and abandoning themselves to that Host of theirs, like clay in God's fashioning hands (Gen 2). This free abandonment to Love created their zeal for acting in the world. And they looked at others with the same worshiping contemplation. Their faith is still a belief in the mystery of the Incarnation two thousand years ago, but it is also a certainty about the presence of Love incarnate in all human beings today. What's more real than *people* around us?

This increasing certainty about God's real presence in all of us does not ignore suffering. Besides practicing the frugality I have described, people for whom God is real have seen themselves and others hurt by life. Their belief, tested in ways I have summarized in this book, is now faith, "assurance of things hoped for, the conviction of things not seen" (Heb 11:1). It has been built through consolations, but also through tears, doubts, and times of darkness, in life and in prayer. People for whom God has become real know that this world will always be, contrary to what all Messianic enthusiasts claim, a panoply of stupid and violent behaviors, but always transfigured by the permanent genesis of Love (Rom 8:22). They have been granted by the Spirit the grace asked by Elisha for his servant: "O Lord, open his eyes, that he may see." Like Elisha seeing God's glory and his call for prophetic ministry in Elijah's death, they discern Love's victory and their call for service in any apparent deadly event (2 Kings 6:17; 2). In simpler words, they know what a friend of mine said to her daughter: "When you fall asleep, don't forget the grain of sand. But, above all, thank God for making a pearl with it."

All of this brings us endlessly back to the Icon of all God's graces, Jesus. This particular Being of Nazareth was

All Possible Universal Love present on earth, and above all in his Passion where everything about Love was said. With deeper faith, those for whom God has become real believe the text of Hebrews about Jesus as the source of salvation, but also see it realized in us today: "In the days of his flesh, Jesus offered up prayers and supplications, with loud cries and tears, to the one who was able to save him from death, and he was heard because of his reverent submission" (Heb 5:7–9). Finally, seeing Love in themselves and others, they praise: "I give you thanks that [we are] wonderfully made"; "Blessed is the one who comes in the name of the Lord! Earth and heaven are full of his glory!" (Ps 139:14; Mt 21:9).

In their certainty, people for whom God has become real are also somehow less and less sure. The deepening of their faith shows them that what they know is nothing compared to what they *don't* know about God. As I was told, they are aware that they face an ocean of mystery. They know what is behind them, but what is ahead of them is a Love limitless and beyond everything, God always Other. This discovery does not disturb them, for it opens on an endless journey of which each stage is a death to the past, but the promise of, and the gate to, a new land. They forget the past for another spring, because they are beckoned by the call of the high sea (Isa 43:18–19).

More and More Respectful

Now, here is the infallible sign that God has become real. People say that it is action, chiefly on behalf of the poor. It is true, for John asserts, "Those who say, 'I love God,' and hate their brothers or sisters, are liars" (1 Jn 4:20). However, this is not sufficient, because all our deeds are always ambiguous. I have seen care for the needy in all people for whom God became real, but *also* an immense respect for nonbelievers and other believers.

This behavior comes directly from what I have just described. God, being greater than all perceptions and religions, is certainly wider than the ways of revelation we know. Therefore, the ones who have experienced God as real don't exclude *anybody* from God's reach and presence. The god of religious fanatics is not real but is often an excuse, projection, justification, and mask for their more or less conscious interests. John is harsh about that: "All who hate a brother or sister are murderers, and you know that murderers do not have eternal life abiding in them" (1 Jn 3:14–15). The "there is no God" of nonbelievers is not a problem for people for whom God is real if they see those nonbelievers accept love as the keystone of everything. For, if persons without religious faith ask us, "Where is your God?" would they say that we are wrong if our answer is: "I believe in Love and we have only this life to promote its reign to happen"? (Ps 14:1; 42:4). Of course, people I am talking about may like or dislike how others might speak about God (or no God) or behave in the name of God (or no God), but they are too aware of Love's infinite mystery in human beings to judge and not to respect *all* of them. "Are we not *all* wonderfully made?" was my thought during the wedding of two not terribly religious friends before a justice of the peace, because no specific church was there claiming property on God-Love (Ps 139:14).

A God Very Real, Because Really Mine

Here is now my last answer to the question of this chapter. We have not learned to pray to a God who is really ours; we have made "the God *of our fathers*" our own (Acts 3:13). Jesus starts like that but goes further. He is *the only one* in the Bible who says to God, "*Abba* [Dad, Daddy]." Having integrated Israel's faith, he molds it with his own experience and calls God with a name of his own. And he teaches us, "When you pray, say — Father." Paul emphasizes that the

Spirit joins our spirit to pray precisely thus, *"Abba"* (Rom 8:14–17). Therefore, *let us pray as Jesus did, literally.*

I know people who experienced unbelievable changes in their relationship with God when they prayed with, "Dad, Daddy." This is difficult for persons whose father was unknown or brutal to them; it was for me because my father was like a void in my childhood. We can use, "Mom, Mommy," but the problem remains the same if our mother was not a strong positive figure in our life. To echo Jesus literally is good, but we can miss the intent of his invitation, which is, "Find a name that is really your own to pray to God with, as *I* did."

This story illustrates that challenge. One day, I invited a bachelor, in directed retreat with me, to pray with "Dad" or "Mom." The next day, noticing the poor result, I suggested, "Use your most tender word." He explained then that it would not be easy to call God "Sweetheart," because he used that word for a woman he loved. Later, he told me this: "In the beginning, I could not say to God 'Sweetheart,' for the face I cherished was always there like a screen. One day, I did it, and God took the essence of the word. *For the first time in my life, at forty-five years of age, I name God with a word that is really my own.* God is no longer others' God, but *my own God.* Also, the masculine images behind 'Father,' or the feminine behind 'Sweetheart,' are gone. God is no longer the victim of my projections. I still cherish Jesus' word, *'Abba,'* for it keeps me in the history of the incarnate God I believe in. But 'Sweetheart' has made God an inexpressible 'genderless' Someone, who has a very unique personal relationship with *me.*" I was so touched that I decided to do the same, and I experienced, with my own name of God, a similar adventure.

Therefore, my answer to the question of this chapter is, "Practice the content of this book. Someday, pray to God with the most tender word of your heart. God will become real for you, will be your own." I have invited many parents and educators to do likewise with children. We must give them the inclination for using the names of Jesus and his God in order to engrave their hearts into the human history of God-Love. With children (or adults, as I did with prisoners) whose parents are unknown or deficient we'll say about *Abba:* "At least, you always have Jesus' God, the Father or the Mother *of all your desires.*" I can testify that this transforms a relationship with God.

But we can suggest, "Name God as Jesus did, but *also* find in your heart the sweetest word of love and use it when you talk to God." Are we afraid to see God prayed to with the nickname of a pet or a baby doll? God, who is not a he or a she, a pet or a baby doll, won't worry about the name used. God will be delighted to be treated with a word full of a very special and personal love. It will even be a marvelous surprise for God, whose name is often misused, to be always called with the deepest tenderness. Finally, a God so real for me as a child won't disappear easily in my adulthood. For it is not a God *borrowed* from others, even in the best conditions; it is *my* God. That is the God of Israel and Jesus, who has become, eventually and definitively, *real for me.*

He Says to His Own, "Let Us Go!" (Jn 14:31)

As I have often mentioned, the content of this book has helped many people to enter into the journey of prayer, with increasing contentment. The adventure was not always easy, but they have never regretted having undertaken that journey. It is still unfinished and full of surprises. If it is always a joy to discover new things about somebody we love and about the love that person has for us; how much more is it in our trip with Jesus' God! And, when we land forever, it will be new again like an everlasting wonder; remember, God is an Ocean. So I hope and trust that this book will help the readers to start and keep sailing, and their children, too. We must just remember Jesus' answer, each time we are going to say, like the fishermen to him, "We have worked all night long but have caught nothing." He said, "Put out into the deep water" (Lk 5:4–5). To go deeper and deeper is price-less because God becomes increasingly real and increasingly mysterious for us. I hope that I have given the reader some-thing like a map for the months and years to come. A map for sailing on the ocean? Yes, somehow. Never mind! When the call of the high sea has been heard once, it can no longer be ignored because it never leaves us. So, I'll end with:

"Bon Voyage!"

Appendix 1

Where Can I Go in Scripture?

This selection might help people to deepen what has touched them and to decode God's message to them through Scriptures.

Meeting a spiritual helper regularly helps prayer life. Indeed, according to what was revealed by the conversation, the helper sometimes suggests to us some passages of Scriptures to pray with. But we don't always have such a person at hand. Also, after years of getting help, we must be able by ourselves to find what we need in the Bible for prayer. This supposes that we know Scripture well enough. The goal of the two following indexes is to help everyone in this search. And the indexes can give spiritual helpers some new suggestions to use.

Praying with our intellect or with a melody is possible with any text. These indexes concern chiefly the method of *contemplation* because it is a traditional and powerful tool for discoveries in prayer; so, they don't aim directly at praying with our intellect, even though they might be helpful for it. Therefore, quotes from Deuteronomy or Leviticus, for instance, won't be found here (the content of such books is usually difficult to contemplate). The psalms are mentioned for the method of praying with a melody — except for praising, for it is easy to find psalms of praise (see Chapter 6, "How Can I Pray? I Don't Know Any Method").

I have quoted only the Old Testament, for two reasons.

1. In the New Testament, the gospels and Acts are familiar to every Christian who wants to contemplate their stories, so I thought it unnecessary to mention them. And, because the texts of the Epistles and Revelation don't easily fit contemplation, I did not include them.

2. I took the Old Testament because a famous scholar told me one day, "If you want to find us with our flesh and blood, go to this part of the Bible." Some people object to the moody God we find in it; through the years, I have discovered that it is a blessing to find there exactly the gods we often carry within ourselves, because of our past wounds. Praying with the Old Testament helps us to get rid of them, because God, there, is *always eventually* merciful and compassionate, forgiving and faithful. And "this" God, emphasized more and more by the texts, blossoms perfectly in Jesus' revelation as Love only. Also, I have selected these texts of the Old Testament, not only because they are well suited to contemplation, but because they have been efficacious for myself and people I have helped (and maybe they are not too well-known by many people).

We should keep in mind that a *theme* includes its opposite. For instance, under *EVIL* we will find passages describing our sinful situation, but also our salvation from sin.

In Index A: When we read just a name like "Jacob," or "David," it means that the whole history of these people has to do with the theme. For the psalms, I am using the Hebrew numbering. Other explanations and references concerning times of ordeal are found in my book *May I Hate God?*

In Index B: "Genesis 1 = p s u v," means that Genesis 1 may be connected with the themes p, s, u, and v. When we have a-d, m-p, it means the themes a, b, c, and d, or the themes m, n, o, and p.

How to Use Index A

Suppose I have been praying with a text of Scripture, and I have experienced a deep feeling of *awe* and *praise*. It was so deep that I suspect something important is there. So I want to stay with my experience and unfold what underlies it and is still unclear. I go to the texts under the theme *rapture,* because *awe,* and *praise* are a part of it. I select among them those that touch me most and pray with them. They may then clarify the first experience, chiefly if this one has lost some of its power. A spiritual helper might guide me to narrow the possible texts.

An example: Isaiah 6:1–8 fills me with awe. I don't understand why. Index A, through the theme *rapture,* sends me to Jonah and eventually Exodus 3. Now, I know: I am called not to escape a situation of injustice, but to be God's compassion for those suffering right where I am.

That is the way of using Index A.

How to Use Index B

While praying with a text, I am deeply touched, but I do not know why. I sense that it is important to understand the reason for such an impact (for instance, I want to answer more consciously a call from God that is still mysterious). I go to Index B. I examine the different themes connected with the particular passage that touched me (my spiritual helper can be useful for such discernment). I discover that one of the themes fits what I have felt. I go back to the themes listed in Index A and find there other texts related to the same theme. I make my selection and pray with the text(s) attracting me, so I can deepen and clarify more consciously what I have begun to discover through the first touch of God.

An example: I am touched by the words of Amos in 7:10–17. I look at the themes connected with this text. The theme "P," *powerlessness,* resounds within me. Eventually, in that theme, Esther 5 strikes me, and I understand: I have to expose myself and intercede for one of my employees.

Therefore, Index B leads back to Index A.

This is not complicated, and I have known spiritual helpers and many other people, laypeople or otherwise, who have used these two indexes efficaciously, and who have expressed gratitude for their usefulness.

Index A

ACCEPTANCE (A)

When I feel accepted or not — as I am, by people, God, and myself. When I accept them (including myself) or not, with *mercy* and *concern, understanding* and *compassion, love.*

    Gen 18:16–33. Ex 2; 3; 32–34. Num 11. 2 Sam 11–12. 1 Kings 17; 19. Esth 5 (Jrslm Bible). Ps 22; 23; 38; 42; 51; 63; 88; 91; 103; 130; 131; 139. Song. Isa 6; 40; 42:1–9; 43:1–7; 49; 50:4–9; 52:13–53:12; 54–55; 60; 61; 62. Jer 1; 18:1–6; 31. Ezek 16; 34; 36; 37. Hos 2; 11:1–9. Hag. Zech 11:4–17.

BELIEF (B)

I feel my *faith* increasing or challenged through events and people. A faith in a loving God, in loving people, and in myself as capable of loving.

    Gen: Abraham; Jacob. Ex 3; 14; 15; 19. Num 11. Josh 6; 24. Judg 6–8. Ruth 1–3. 1 Sam 3; 17. 2 Sam 7. 1 Kings 3; 10; 17; 19. 2 Kings 4; 5. Esth (Jrslm B.) 5. Ps 8; 22; 23; 63; 91; 103; 130; 131; 139. Song. Isa 6; 40; 43:1–7; 49; 50:4–9; 52:13–53:12; 54–55; Jer 1; 18:1–16; 31; Ezek 16; 37; 47. Dan 7:9–14. Hos 2; 11:1–9. Am 7:10–17. Mic 6:8. Hab 2:1–2.

COMPANIONSHIP (C)

In a situation, I feel called to *brotherhood/sisterhood,* with people or *companionship* with God, with its joys and problems.

Gen 1–2; Abraham; Jacob. Ex 3; 32–34. Num 11. Josh 1; 24. Judg 6–8. Ruth 1–3. 1 Sam 16; 17; David. 2 Sam 1:25–27. 1 Kings 19. Esth (Jrslm Bible) 5. Ps 22; 23. Song. Isa 5:1–7; 6; 40; 42:1–9; 43:1–7; 49:14–16; 52:13–53:12; 54–55; 60; 61; 62. Jer 1; 31. Ezek 16; 34; 36. Dan 7:9–14. Hos 2; 11:1–9; Am 2:6–16; 6. Jon. Hag. Zech 11:4–17

DANGER (D)

I feel that I am full of *fear,* even because of God.

Ex 3; 14; 32–34. Josh 1. 1 Sam 17. 1 Kings 19. Esth (Jrslm Bible) 5. Ps 22; 23; 38; 51; 88; 91; 103; 130; 139. Song. Isa 6; 43:1–7; 50:4–9; 52:13–53:12; 54–55; 60; 61; 62. Jer 1; 31. Ezek 16; 27–28; 37; 47. Hos 2; 11:1–9. Am 7:10–17. Jon. Mic 6:8. Hab 2:1–4. Hag.

EVIL (E)

I feel that I am *put to the test* or dealing with *evil, sin, temptation.*

Gen 3; 4; 11:1–10. Ex 14; 32–34. 1 Sam 17; David. 2 Sam 11–12. 1 Kings 19. Ps 22; 38; 51; 88; 91; 103; 130; 131. Isa 6; 40; 42:1–9; 50:4–9; 52:13–53:12; 54–55; 61. Jer 31. Ezek 16; 27–28; 34; 36; 37. Hos 2; 11:1–9. Am 2:6–16; 6. Jon. Hag. Zech 11:4–17.

FIGHT (F)

I feel in *conflict* with people, myself (with God, see *wrestling*).

Gen 4; 21; 22. Jacob. Ex 14; 32–34. Num 11; 22–24. Josh 1; 6. Judg 11:29–40. 1 Sam 17; David. 1 Kings 3; 19. Ps 22; 38; 51; 88; 91; 139. Song. Isa 42:1–9; 43:1–7; 49; 50:4–9; 52:13–53:12; 54–55; 60; 61; 62. Jer 1; 18:1–6; 31. Ezek 2–3; 16; 27–28; 34; 36. Hos 2; 11:1–9. Am 2:6–16; 6. Jon. Hag. Zech 11:4–17.

Guest (G)

I feel called to *hospitality* of heart, *to welcome* anybody without any discrimination, to welcome God. Maybe I am unable to do so.

Gen 18:1–15. Ex 32–34. Josh 24. Ruth 1–3. 1 Sam 3; 16; David. 2 Sam 6. 2 Kings 4; 5. Ps 23; 63; 103; 131; 139. Song. Isa 40; 42:1–9; 49; 50:4–9; 52:13–53:12; 54–55; 60; 62. Jer 1; 18:1–6. Ezek 2–3; 16; 27–28; 36; 37; 47. Dan 7:9–14. Hos 2; 11:1–9. Am 2:6–16; 6; 7:10–17. Jon. Mic 6:8. Hab 2:1–4. Hag.

Human (Being) (H)

When I feel my *human condition* (with its *freedom* and *limitations*), called to *action* or *passivity,* in order to let God act freely.

Gen 1–3; 11; Jacob. Ex 14; 32. Josh 24. Judg 6–8. Ruth 1–3. 1 Sam 17. 2 Sam 11–12. 2 Kings 5. 1 Chr 29. Ps 1; 8; 38; 51; 63; 88; 91; 103; 131; 139. Song. Isa 6; 43:1–7; 54–55. Jer 1; 18:1–6. Ezek 2–3; 16; 27–28; 34. Hos 2; 11:1–9. Am 2:6–16; 6. Jon. Mic 6:8. Hag.

Intercession (I)

My heart wants to intercede for people (or suffers because I don't). I feel that I need an *intercession.* Some texts here are just about some prayers.

Gen 18:16–33. Ex 32–34. Num 11. Josh 1. 1 Kings 10; 19. Esth (Jrslm Bible) 5. Ps 22; 23; 38; 51; 63; 88; 91; 103; 130; 139. Song. Isa 6; 42:1–9; 43:1–7; 49; 50:4–9; 52:13–53:12; 54–55; 61; 62. Jer 31. Ezek 16; 37. Hos 11:1–9. Jon. Hag.

Joining (J)

I feel the joy and difficulty *to communicate,* a desire or a reluctance to do so, with others, God included.

Gen 11:1–10; Jacob. Ex 19; 32–34. 1 Sam 3. 1 Kings 10; 19. Esth (Jrslm B.) 5. Ps 22; 38; 42; 51; 63; 88; 91; 103; 130;

139. Song. Isa 42:1–9; 43:1–7; 49; 50:4–9; 52:13–53:12; 54–55; 61; 62. Jer 1; 31. Ezek 2–3; 16; 36. Hos 2; 11:1–9. Am 2:6–16; 6; 7:10–17. Jon. Mic 6:8. Hab 2:1–4.

KILLING (K)

When I feel myself in a situation of *suffering, agony, anxiety,* or *death,* called (with attraction or repulsion) to be with the *suffering Christ.* And, through that, I feel or do not feel the presence of *life.*

Gen 4; 22; Joseph. Ex 14; 32:30–35. Num 11. Judg 11:29–40. 1 Sam 17. 1 Kings 17; 19. Ps 22; 38; 42; 51; 88; 91; 103; 130; 139. Song. Isa 42:1–9; 43:1–7; 49; 50:4–9; 52:13–53:12; 54–55; 60; 61. Jer 31. Ezek 16; 37. Hos 2. Am 2:6–16; 6; 7:10–17. Jon. Hag. Zech 11:4–17.

LISTENING (L)

I feel invited to be *just present, listening,* and *silent;* or to hear the Lord and, maybe, *discern.*

Ex 3; 19. Ruth 1–3. 1 Sam 3; 16. 1 Kings 3; 10; 19. Ps 103; 131; 139. Song. Isa 6; 42:1–9; 43:1–7; 49; 50:4–9; 52:13–53:12; 54–55. Jer 1. Ezek 2–3; 16; 36. Hos 2; 11:1–9. Am 7:10–17. Jon. Mic 6:8. Hab 2:1–4. Hag.

MAN-WOMAN (M)

Situations involve *relationship, friendship,* or *love,* and I feel that something there might concern my *sexuality.*

Gen 1–3; 21; 24; Jacob. Judg 11:29–40; 14–16. Ruth 1–3. 1 Sam 17. 2 Sam 1:25–27; 6:11–12. 1 Kings 3:16–28; 10; 17; 19. Tob. Esth (Jrslm B.) 5. Ps 1; 63; 103; 131; 139. Prov 8:22–31. Song. Isa 5:1–7; 6; 43:1–7; 54–55; 60; 62. Jer 1; 18:1–6; 31. Ezek 2–3; 16; 34; 36; 37; 47. Hos 2:11:1–9.

NURSING (N)

A situation gives me feelings of *care, healing, forgiveness,* and *salvation.*

Gen: Joseph. Ex 2; 3; 14; 32–34. Num 11. Josh 1. Judg 6–8. Ruth 1–3. 1 Sam 24; 26; David. 2 Sam 11–12. 1 Kings 17. 2 Kings 4; 5. Ps 8; 22; 23; 38; 42; 51; 63; 88; 91; 103; 130; 139. Song. Isa 5:1–7; 6; 40; 42:1–9; 43:1–7; 49; 50:4–9; 52:13–53:12; 54–55; 60; 61; 62. Jer 18:1–6; 31. Ezek 16; 27–28; 34; 36; 37; 47. Hos 2; 11:1–9. Am 2:6–16; 6. Jon.

OFFERING (O)

I feel called *to offer* what I have and who I am, or I am refusing.
Gen 12:1–9; Abraham; Jacob. Ex 3; 14; 32–34. Josh 1; 24. Judg 6–8. Ruth 1–3. 1 Sam 3; 16. 2 Sam 7. 1 Kings 3; 10; 19. 2 Kings 5. 1 Chr 29. Ps 63; 103; 139. Song. Isa 5:1–7; 6; 42:1–9; 43:1–7; 49; 50:4–9; 52:13–53:12; 54–55; 60; 61; 62. Jer 1; 18:1–6; 31. Ezek 2–3; 16; 34; 36; 37; 47. Dan 7:9–14. Hos 2; 11:1–9. Jon. Mic 6:8. Hab 2:1–4. Hag. Zech 11:4–17.

POWERLESSNESS (P)

I experience or refuse *powerlessness.*
Gen 32. Ex 3; 14. Josh 1. Judg 6–8. Ruth 1–3. 1 Sam 16; 17; David. 1 Kings 3; 17; 19. 2 Kings 4; 5. 1 Chr 29. Esth (Jrslm B.) 5. Ps 22; 38; 42; 51; 63; 88; 91; 103; 131; 139. Song. Isa 42:1–9; 43:1–7; 49; 50:4–9; 52:13–53:12; 54–55; 60; 61; 62. Jer 1; 18:1–6. Ezek 2–3; 16; 36; 37; 47. Hos 2; 11:1–9. Am 7:10–17. Jon. Hab 2:1–4. Hag. Zech 11:4–17.

QUEST (Q)

I feel myself as *looking for* God and/or *being looked for* by God.
Gen: Jacob. Ex 3; 14; 19; 32–34. Num 11:24–30. Josh 1. Ruth 1–3. 1 Sam 3. 1 Kings 3; 10; 19. 2 Kings 5. Esth (Jrslm B.) 5. Ps 22; 23; 42; 63; 103; 130; 131; 139. Song. Isa 5:1–7; 6; 40; 43:1–7; 49; 50:4–9; 52:13–53:12; 54–55; 60; 61; 62. Jer 1; 31. Ezek 2–3; 16; 34; 36; 37; 47. Dan 7:9–14. Hos 2;

11:1–9. Am 7:10–17. Jon. Mic 6:8. Hab 2:1–4. Hag. Zech 11:4–17.

RAPTURE (R)

God's *mystery* and *action* create within me *awe, praise, adoration.*

Gen 15; 18; 32; Abraham; Jacob. Ex 3; 14; 19; 32–34. Num 11:24–30. Josh 1. Judg 6–8. 2 Sam 6. 1 Kings 19. Ps 8; 22; 103; 139. Song. Isa 6; 42:1–9; 43:1–7; 50:4–9; 52:13–53:12; 54–55; 60; 61; 62. Jer 1; 18:1–6; 31. Ezek 2–3; 16; 36; 37; 47. Dan 7:9–14. Hos 2; 11:1–9. Jon.

SACRIFICE (S)

I feel that life asks me for a *sacrifice* that I accept or not.

Gen 22; 32. Ex 14. Judg 11:29–40. 1 Kings 19. 2 Kings 4. 1 Chr 29. Ps 22; 51; 103. Isa 6; 42:1–9; 43:1–7; 50:4–9; 52:13–53:12; 54–55; 61; 62. Ezek 16; 27–28. Hos 2. Am 2:6–16; 6; 7:10–17. Jon.

(GIVING) THANKS (T)

I feel I need *to thank,* or am called to *playfulness.*

Num 11. Josh 1. 1 Kings 10. 1 Chr 29. Esth (Jrslm B.) 5. Ps 8; 23; 63; 103; 139. Prov 8:22–31. Song. Isa 6; 40; 42:1–9; 43:1–7; 49; 50:4–9; 52:13–53:12; 54–55; 60; 61; 62. Jer 1; 31. Ezek 16; 36; 37; 47. Hos 2; 11:1–9. Am 7:10–17. Jon. Hag. Zech 11:4–17.

UNION (U)

I feel *one* with God, or called to a *covenant,* a *promise* filling me with *hope.* Or I feel myself as doubting all of that.

Gen 12:1–9; 15; 28:10–22; 32; Abraham; Jacob. Ex 3; 14; 19; 32–34. Num 11:24–30. Josh 1; 24. Ruth 1–3. 1 Sam 16. 2 Sam 7. 1 Kings 10; 19. 2 Kings 5. 1 Chr 29. Esth (Jrslm B.) 5. Ps 8; 22; 23; 42; 63; 103; 131; 139. Song. Isa 5:1–7; 6; 40; 42:1–9; 43:1–7; 49; 50:4–9; 52:13–53:12; 54–55; 60; 61; 62.

Jer 1; 18:1–6; 31. Ezek 2–3; 16; 36; 37; 47. Dan 7:9–14. Hos 2; 11:1–9. Am 7:10–17. Mic 6:8. Hab 2:1–4. Hag.

VIOLENCE (V)

I feel *violence* of any kind, from or against people or myself.

Gen 3–4; Jacob; Joseph. Ex 14; 32–34. Num 22–24. Judg 6–8; 11:29–40. 1 Sam 17; 24; 26. 2 Sam 11–12. 1 Kings 19. Ps 22; 23; 38; 42; 51; 63; 88; 91; 103; 130. Song. Isa 40; 42:1–9; 43:1–7; 50:4–9; 52:13–53:12; 54–55; 60; 61; 62. Jer 18:1–6. Ezek 16; 27–28; 34; 36; 37. Hos 2; 11:1–9. Am 2:6–16; 6; 7:10–17. Jon. Hag. Zech 11:4–17.

WRESTLING (W)

When I feel like *struggling* with God, or feel God struggling with me.

Gen 32. Ex 14; 32–34. Num 11. Josh 24. Judg 6–8; 11:29–40. Ruth 1–3. 1 Sam 1–2; 17. 1 Kings 10; 19. 2 Kings 4; 5. 1 Chr 29. Esth (Jrslm B.) 5. Ps 22; 42; 51; 63; 88; 91; 103; 130; 131; 139. Prov 8:22–31. Song. Isa 5:1–7; 6; 42:1–9; 50:4–9; 52:13–53:12; 54–55; 60; 61; 62. Jer 1; 18:1–6. Ezek 2–3; 16; 27–28; 37; 47. Hos 2; 11:1–9. Am 7:10–17. Jon.

X-(RAY) (X)

I feel I am dealing with my *self-image,* which I accept or not, judge as good or bad.

Gen 1–3; Jacob. Num 11:24–30. Judg 6–8; 11:29–40. Ruth 1–3. 1 Sam 1–2; 16; 17; David. 1 Kings 10; 19. 2 Kings 5. 1 Chr 29. Esth (Jrslm B.) 5. Ps 8; 22; 23; 38; 42; 51; 63; 88; 91; 103; 130; 131; 139. Prov 8:22–31. Song. Isa 5:1–7; 6; 40; 42:1–9; 43:1–7; 49; 50:4–9; 52:13–53:12; 54–55; 60; 61; 62. Jer 1; 18:1–6; 31. Ezek 2–3; 16; 27–28; 34; 36; 37; 47. Dan 7:9–14. Hos 2; 11:1–9. Am 2:6–16; 7:10–17. Jon. Mic 6:8. Hag. Zech 11:4–17.

YEARNING (Y)

I feel myself thirsty in a kind of *desert, longing for*...

Gen 21. Ex 32–34. 1 Kings 17; 19. Ps 22; 42; 103; 139. Song. Isa 40; 42:1–9; 43:1–7; 49; 50:4–9; 52:13–53:12; 54–55; 60; 61; 62. Jer 31. Ezek 16; 37; 47. Hos 2. Jon. Hab 2:1–4. Hag.

ZERO (POINT) (Z)

I feel a *beginning,* starting a *new life,* or *leaving*... I feel that I don't want to do so.

Gen 12:1–9; 25:19–25; Abraham; Jacob. Ex 3; 14; 32–34. Josh 1; 24. Judg 6–8. Ruth 1–3. 1 Sam 3; 16; 17. 2 Sam 7. 1 Kings 3; 10; 19. 2 Kings 5. 1 Chr 29. Ps 22; 42; 51; 91; 103; 139. Song. Isa 6; 40; 42:1–9; 43:1–7; 50:4–9; 52:13–53:12; 54–55; 60; 61; 62. Jer 1; 18:1–6; 31. Ezek 2–3; 16; 36; 37; 47. Dan 7:9–14. Hos 2; 11:1–9. Am 7:10–17. Jon. Mic 6:8. Hab 2:1–4. Hag.

Index B

(in alphabetical order, in order to make the search easier)

AMOS (AM)

    2:6–16 = C E-H J K N S V X

1 CHRONICLES (1 CHR)

    29 = H O P S-U W Y Z

DANIEL (DAN)

    7:9–14 = B C G I O Q R U X Z

ESTHER (ESTH) (JERUSALEM BIBLE)

    5 = A-D H-J M P Q T U W X

EXODUS (EX)

    2 = A N
    3 = A-D L N-R U Z
    14–15 = B-F H K N-S U-W Z
    19 = B J L Q R U
    32–34 = A C-G I-K N O Q R U-Z

EZEKIEL (EZEK)

    2–3 = F-H J L M O-R U W X Z
    16 = A-Z
    27–28 = D-H N S V-X
    34 = A C E F H M-O Q V X

```
36 = A-C E-G J L-R T-V X Z
37 = A B D E G I K M-R T-Z
47 = B D G M-R T U W-Z
```

GENESIS (GEN)

```
1–3 = C H M X
3–4 = E F K V
11:1–10 = E H J
12:1–9 = O U Z
15 = R U
18 = A I G R
21 = F M Y
22 = F J S
25:19–25 = Z
28:10–22 = U
32 = P R S U W
Abraham = B C O R U Z
Jacob = B C F H J M O Q R U V X Z
Joseph = K N V
```

HABAKKUK (HAB)

```
2:1–4 = B D G J L N-Q U Y Z
```

HAGGAI (HAG)

```
A-I K L N-Q T-V X-Z
```

HOSEA (HOS)

```
2 = A-H J-Z
11:1–9 = A-J L-R T-Z
```

ISAIAH (ISA)

```
5:1–7 = C M-O Q U W Z
6 = A-E I L-O Q-T U W X Z
40 = A-C E G N Q T-U X-Z
```

42:1–9 = A C E-H I-L N-P R-Z
43:1–7 = A-F H-Z
49 = A-C E-G I-Q T U X Y
50:4–9 = A B D-G I-L N-Z
52:13–53:12 = A-G I-L N-Z
54–55 = A-Z
60 = A C D F G K M-R T-Z
61 = A-F I-K N-Z
62 = A C-G I J M-Z

Jeremiah (Jer)

1 = A-D F-H J L M O-R T U W X Z
18:1–6 = A B F-H M-P R U-X Z
31 = A-F I-K M-O Q R T U X-Z

Judges (Judg)

6–8 = B C H N-P R V-X Z
11:29–40 = F K M S V-X
14–16 = M

Jonah (Jon)

C-L N-T V-Z

Joshua (Josh)

1 = C D F I N-R T U Z
6 = B F
24 = B C G H O U W Z

1 Kings (1 Kings)

3 = B F L M O-Q Z
10 = B J L M O Q T U W X Z
17 = A B I K M N P Y
19 = A-F I-S U-Z

2 Kings (2 Kings)

> 4 = B G N P S V W Z
> 5 = B G H N-Q U W X Z

Micah (Mic)

> 6:8 = B D G H J L O Q U X Z

Numbers (Num)

> 11 = A-C F G I K N Q R T U W X Z
> 22–24 = F H L V X

Proverbs (Prov)

> 8:22–31 = M Y W X

Psalms (Ps)

> 1 = H M
> 8 = B H N R T U X
> 22 = A-F I-K N P Q S U V-Y
> 23 = A-D G I N Q T-V X
> 38 = A D-F H-K N P V X
> 42 = A J K N P Q U-Z
> 51 = A D-F H-K N P S V X Z
> 63 = A B G-J M-Q T-X
> 88 = A D-F H-K N P V-X
> 91 = A B D-F H-K N P V-X Z
> 103 = A B D E G-Z
> 130 = A B D E I-K N P Q V-X
> 131 = A B E G H L-N P Q U W X
> 139 = A B D-R T U W-Z

Ruth (Ruth)

> 1–3 = B C G H L-Q U W X Z

1 SAMUEL (1 SAM)

1–2 = M W X
3 = B G J L O Q Z
16 = C G L O P U X Z
17 = B-F H K M P V-X Z
24 = N V
26 = N V
David = C E-G N P X

2 SAMUEL (2 SAM)

1:25–27 = C M
6 = G M R
7 = B O U Z
11–12 = A E H M N V X

SONG OF SONGS (SONG)

A-D F-J L-R T-Z

TOBIT (TOB) M

ZECHARIAH (ZECH)

11:4–17 = A C E F K N-Q T V X

Appendix 2

Scriptures Cited in This Book

About the Author...

Born in Marseilles, France, Pierre Wolff is a former Jesuit priest with advanced degrees in Philosophy and Theology who now ministers to the Episcopal diocese in Wallingford, Connecticut, where he resides. A popular retreat director and seminar leader in the United States and France, Wolff is also a noted teacher of discernment and Ignatian spirituality.

Wolff's previous books include *God's Passion, Our Passion, Discernment: The Art of Choosing Well, Is God Deaf?,* and *May I Hate God?*